D1614575

The Color of Melancholy

PARALLAX RE-VISIONS OF CULTURE
AND SOCIETY

Stephen G. Nichols, Gerald Prince, and Wendy Steiner
SERIES EDITORS

The Color of Melancholy

The Uses of Books in the Fourteenth Century

Jacqueline Cerquiglini-Toulet

TRANSLATED BY
Lydia G. Cochrane

The Johns Hopkins University Press
Baltimore and London

Publication of this volume was supported by grants from
the Centre Louis Marin, The Johns Hopkins University,
and the French Ministry of Culture.

Originally published as *La Couleur de la mélancolie: La
fréquentation des livres au XIVᵉ siècle 1300–1415,* © 1993
Hatier, Paris. Published by arrangement with Hatier, Paris.

Printed in the United States of America on acid-free paper
06 05 04 03 02 01 00 99 98 97   5 4 3 2 1

Illustrations reproduced with the permission of the
Walters Art Gallery, Baltimore, Maryland, from *Medieval
and Renaissance Manuscripts in the Walters Art Gallery,*
by Lilian M. C. Randall (Baltimore: Johns Hopkins
University Press, 1992). © 1992, The Walters Art Gallery.

The Johns Hopkins University Press
2715 North Charles Street
Baltimore, Maryland 21218-4319
The Johns Hopkins Press Ltd., London

Library of Congress Cataloging-in-Publication Data will
be found at the end of this book.
A catalog record for this book is available from the
British Library.
ISBN 0-8018-5381-8

This book was born of friendship and written in friendship. My thanks, from start to finish, to Michel Chaillou. My thanks also to the University of Geneva, Charles Méla, dean of the Faculty of Letters, and to Colette Isoz and Olivier Collet.

Escollier de Merencolye,
Des verges de Soussy batu,
Je suis a l'estude tenu,
Es derreniers jours de ma vye.

Charles d'Orléans

Contents

Illustrations

Foreword

The Author, the Book, and Literature

Roger Chartier

In a famous essay, Michel Foucault asked, "What is an author?" Or, rather, he raised questions about the conditions and mechanisms that have led us to the habit of assigning a proper name to a literary text and to link the work with the writer who originated it. In their quest for the moment in which these founding categories of the modern concept of literature was formed, historians have tended to stress two high points in time: the eighteenth century, when the notion of literary property arose, and the sixteenth century, with its censorship, by churches and states, of authors held to be heterodox.

Jacqueline Cerquiglini-Toulet's elegant and subtle book obliges us to stretch our retrospective gaze beyond those two moments. As her *chemin de longue étude* through French literature of the fourteenth century—a century that came to an end with Agincourt—invites us to consider, it was in that century, unloved by literary criticism, that the figure of the author was invented. Signs of this abound. The first was in language, with the new meanings attributed to the words *écrivain,* designating the person who composes a work as well as one who copies a book, and *invention,* which, with the early years of the fifteenth century, had come to mean an original human creation rather than solely the happy discovery of what God, the sole *droit créateur,* had produced. The second sign was in the book, with miniature portraits of the writer, often pictured in the process of writing (in both senses of the word *écrire*). A traditional depiction of *auctoritates*—ancient authors or Fathers of the Church—was thus shifted to contemporary writers who expressed themselves in French rather than in Latin and who composed poems, romances, and histories rather than theological tomes, juridical encyclopedias, or "mirrors of the world."

Two major transformations accompanied this new notion of invention. One concerned texts, the other, books. In the fourteenth century, a time of concern that poetic material was drying up and inspiration becoming exhausted—Jean Le Fèvre wrote in 1376 that there was nothing new under the sun—writing, letters, and the book became the subject matter of works aimed at entertaining or teaching. "Literature" was born of that return of writing onto itself, of that effort to constitute a repertory of genres and a canon for "moderns." In the cemetery in René d'Anjou's *Livre du Cuer d'Amours espris,* six graves "not far from the others but as if set apart" recall the "most excellent" poets: Ovid, Guillaume de Machaut, Giovanni Boccaccio, Jean de Meun, Petrarch, and Alain Chartier—four of them fourteenth-century authors (141).

This *mise en abyme* of the creative act, reflected in literary creation itself, took several forms. It brought narratives about the mythical inventors of writing: Orpheus the magician, Thoth the scribe, and Cadmus and Carmentis (also called Nicostrata)—a female figure among male heroes—credited, respectively, with the introduction of alphabetic writing in Greece and the invention of Latin letters. It also inspired the first funerary eulogy by a writer to the memory of another poet whom he recognized as his master, the two ballades Eustache Deschamps wrote to Guillaume de Machaut.

Along with literature came the book. That is not to say that the fourteenth century invented the book as the principal form for fixing and transmitting the literary text. In the last centuries of the Middle Ages, the book already had a long past, going back to the substitution of the *codex* for the roll somewhere between the second and fourth centuries of the Christian era. What was new was the alliance set up among the book, the work, and the author. The traditional and durable form of a commonplace book, a collection of texts of varying genres, dates, and authorship that a reader copied or had copied and bound into one *codex* volume, found a rival in a new conception of the manuscript, henceforth understood as a book offering the works of one author or perhaps only one work. This was a somewhat paradoxical development in an age in which writing was often thought of as compilation or reuse and in which its most frequent image (to the point of becoming a worn topos) was that of the gleaner gathering up strands of grain left by the great harvesters of the past. The unity established between the material integrity of the book and the singularity of the works that came from the same pen clearly shows that some authors of the time who wrote in the vernacular enjoyed the same "codicological dignity" as the older authorities.

The fourteenth century, a disenchanted and melancholic age haunted by the impermanence of things and the fragility of words and one that lastingly associated writing with death, was nonetheless a time of inventions fundamental for written works in the vernacular: the invention of the author as the creator of a work that expressed his or her unique genius, the invention of literature as an object for reflection and as the very matter of the poetic gesture, and the invention of the book as a means for presenting the work and the author in their full individuality.

Readers did not change their practices at the same pace, and the century saw no real revolution in reading. Throughout her book, Jacqueline Cerquiglini-Toulet offers valuable insights about a dual reality. On the one hand, she presents evidence that reading aloud remained a deep-rooted and widespread habit. This could be a poet reading to a prince, as with Jean Froissart reading his *Meliador* to Gaston Phoebus or it could be the poet who was the listener. Froissart himself states, "Throughout my life, I seldom let a day of leisure pass by, when I was in good health, without reading, writing, meditating on letters, *hearing someone read,* or questioning those who kept silent." On the other hand, she confirms the notion that private, silent, and purely visual reading, formerly practiced only in the monasteries, then in the schools and universities, became a common practice among the rulers and elites in the fourteenth century. This is demonstrated, in one of the last texts given in the book, by the reaction of King Richard II of England to the book of poems that the same Froissart offered him: "[Il] regarda dedens le livre en plusieurs lieux et y lisy, car moult bien parloit et lisoit de franchois" [He was delighted, and read out several of the poems, for he read and spoke French fluently]. The use of books in the fourteenth century, as later, in the early modern age, was thus, for the lettered, alternatively participation as a member of a group listening to a text being read and the more secret pleasure of a text enjoyed in the silence of a private retreat.

A book of literature on literature and a magnificent example of the exercise of criticism at its best, Jacqueline Cerquiglini-Toulet's *Color of Melancholy* makes an essential contribution to the area of scholarly work and reflection in recent years that has brought together in one history the study of works, the description of their material forms, and a comprehension of the various meanings invested in them by their authors, their copyists or printers, and their readers. In this respect, this book is faithful to the writers it invites us to come to know and to love. For them, too, literary invention could not be separated from the books that kept its trace and its memory.

Historical and Literary Chronology of the Fourteenth Century

ca. 1300	Birth of Guillaume de Machaut.
1305	Founding of the Collège de Navarre, "cradle of French humanism," by the will of Jeanne de Navarre, the wife of Philippe le Bel.
1307	Dante begins the *Divine Comedy*.
1309	Installation of Pope Clement V (of French origin) at Avignon.
1312	Jacques de Longuyon writes *Les Voeux du Paon*.
ca. 1320	William of Occam teaches at Paris.
1321	Death of Dante.
1322–24	Decretal of Pope John XXII to denounce the supposed abuses of the *Ars nova*.
1324	Marsilius of Padua, with Jean de Jandun, completes the *Defensor pacis,* sustaining the authority of the councils over that of the pope.
1327	Birth of Philippe de Mézières.
before 1328	The *Ovide moralisé* is written.

1328	Philippe de Valois becomes king of France as Philip VI.
	Shift from the Capetian dynasty to the Valois dynasty.
	Poèmes of Watriquet de Couvin.
1331	Guillaume de Digulleville, *Le Pèlerinage de la vie humaine.*
1332	Jean Acart de Hesdin, *La Prise amoureuse.*
1335	Philippe de Vitry, *Le Chapel des Trois Fleurs de Lis.*
1337	King Edward III of England claims the French crown.
	Start of what later was known as the Hundred Years' War, which began as a war of succession and ended as a war between nations.
	Birth of Jean Froissart.
	Death of Giotto.
1340	Birth of Geoffrey Chaucer.
	Condemnation at Paris of the ideas of William of Occam.
1341	Petrarch crowned poet laureate at Rome.
1342	Works of Jean de Le Mote.
1346	August: Defeat of Philip VI at Crécy.
	Birth of Eustache Deschamps.
	Guillaume de Machaut, *Le Jugement dou roy de Behaingne.*
1348	The Black Death.
1349	Death of William of Occam.
	Guillaume de Machaut, *Le Jugement dou roy de Navarre.*
	Boccaccio writes *The Decameron.*
1350	Accession of John II (Jean le Bon), king of France.
1352	Death of Gilles Li Muisis.
1356	September 19: Battle of Poitiers.
	Jean le Bon taken prisoner.

1357	Guillaume de Machaut, *Le Confort d'Ami,* written for Charles de Navarre.
	Guillaume de Digulleville, *Le Pèlerinage de l'âme.*
	Petrarch, *I Trionfi.*
1358	Revolt and death of Etienne Marcel.
	The Jacquerie.
1360	Treaty of Brétigny: Jean le Bon freed in exchange for hostages, among them his sons (excluding the dauphin).
1361	Froissart's first trip to England.
1362	Guillaume de Machaut begins the *Voir-Dit.*
1363	Birth of Jean Gerson.
	Birth of Nicolas de Clamanges.
1364	April 8: Death of Jean le Bon.
	Accession of Charles V; crowned at Reims on May 19.
1365	Christine de Pizan born at Venice.
1370	Du Guesclin named *connétable.*
	Jean Froissart begins his *Chroniques.*
	Jean Le Fèvre translates the *Lamentations* of Matheolus.
1373	Boccaccio, *De genealogia deorum.*
1374	July 18: Petrarch dies as he had wished, his head lying on the Virgil manuscript he was copying.
1375	Death of Boccaccio.
1377	Death of Guillaume de Machaut.
	Jean Gerson enters the Collège de Navarre.
1378	Beginning of the Great Schism: two popes, Urban VI and Robert of Geneva, who takes the name Clement VII.
1379	Clement VII established at Avignon.
1380	July: Death of Du Guesclin.
	September 16: Death of Charles V.

	November 4: Charles VI crowned.
	Philippe de Mézières retires to the Celestine monastery in Paris.
1381	Death of Jan van Ruysbroek, whose mysticism inspired the *devotio moderna* and influenced Jean Gerson.
1382	Maillotins uprising at Paris.
	Death of Nicole Oresme.
1384	Jean Froissart, *Meliador.*
1385	July 17: Marriage of Charles VI and Isabeau of Bavaria.
1387	Philippe de Mézières, *Griseldis.*
	Geoffrey Chaucer, *Canterbury Tales.*
1389	Pierre d'Ailly chancelor of the University of Paris.
1392	August 5: Charles VI's first fit of madness.
	Eustache Deschamps, *L'Art de dictier.*
1393	January: Bal des Ardents.
1394	Birth of Charles d'Orléans, oldest son of Louis, duc d'Orléans, and Valentine Visconti.
	Christine de Pizan begins to write the *Cent Ballades.*
1395	Jean Gerson succeeds Pierre d'Ailly as chancellor of the University of Paris.
1396	September 25: Catastrophic defeat of combined western European forces by the Turks at Nicopolis.
1397	Death of Oton de Grandson in a duel at Bourg-en-Bresse.
1400	Laurent de Premierfait translates Boccaccio, *De casibus virorum.*
1401	Institution of the Cour d'Amour of Charles VI.
1402	*Querelle* of the *Roman de la Rose.*
1404	Christine de Pizan, *Le Livre de la mutacion de fortune.*

1405	Death of Philippe de Mézières at nearly eighty years of age.

Epistre of Christine de Pizan to Isabeau of Bavaria, queen of France. |
| 1407 | November 23: Assassination of Louis d'Orléans by order of Jean sans Peur, duke of Burgundy. |
| 1410 | Jacques Legrand, *Le Livre des bonnes meurs.*

Christine de Pizan, *Lamentacion sur les maux de la France.* |
| 1414 | Opening of the Council of Constance. |
| 1415 | July 6: Jan Hus burned at the stake at Constance for heresy.

October 25: Agincourt, Charles d'Orléans taken prisoner. |
| 1418 | End of the schism of the Western Church.

Death of Jean de Montreuil at the Burgundians' entry into Paris.

Massacre of the Armagnacs. |
| 1419 | September 10: Assassination of Jean sans Peur at Montereau. |

The Color of Melancholy

1 | Through the Eyes of a Monk

In 1350, Gilles Li Muisis, a Benedictine who had just lost his sight and who, at seventy-eight, was an old man, looked back at his past. What is more, this monk, who had little background in literature (he had entered the monastery of Saint-Martin in Tournai at the age of eighteen), began to write. He tells us that he read authors of the preceding century: among them, the works of another monk, Le Reclus de Molliens:

> Des viers dou Reclus que diroie?
> Que moult volentiers, se pooie,
> Les liroie trestous les jours.
>
> (Li Méditations, in Poésies, 1:86–87)[1]

> [What shall I say of the Hermit's poems? That if I could I would willingly read them every day.]

Next, he read *Le Roman de la Rose:* "J'ai pau trouvet plus bielle chose" [I have rarely found anything more beautiful]. He admired contemporary writers: Guillaume de Machaut, Philippe de Vitry,

---

1. Page indications correspond to the editions listed in the bibliography. The English translations are based on the author's renderings into modern French unless otherwise credited.

Jean de Le Mote. Aside from the *Roman de la Rose,* Gilles was also familiar with works from Champagne and Picardy.

Gilles's reading list provides a picture of the literature of the time, as drawn up in Tournai in a new indulgence year. The times were so hard—filled with war, plague, famines, and all manner of social upheaval—that people had much to be pardoned for. When the hundred-year interval for the Jubilee years proclaimed by the popes was halved, Eustache Deschamps noted the reasons for the change "de cinquante ans en cinquante ans a Romme" [from fifty years to fifty years at Rome]:

> Qui par avant et d'ancienneté
> Fut a cent ans, mais pour l'abregement
> De nostre aage et la fragilité,
> L'a accourcy.
> (*Oeuvres complètes,* 8:203, no. 1490, ll. 11–14)

> [What before and for all time had been set at one hundred years, because of the shortness and fragility of our lives «the pope» has shortened.]

In 1300, Gilles Li Muisis had made the pilgrimage to Rome: "Bien le puis tiesmoignier, car là pérégrinay" (*Li Estas des Papes,* in *Poésies,* 1:304) [Well can I testify, for I went there in pilgrimage]. Another pardon year came in 1350.

At Avignon, Petrarch, a poet—what is more, a poet laureate—stood in judgment of French literature. A good many poets were crowned with laurels in that century, on the Capitoline at Rome but also in the *puys* of the cities and towns of northern France—literary and festive associations where jongleurs and burghers mingled. Gilles Li Muisis says of one author, Collart Haubert, about whom little else is known:

> Es puis l'a on la couronnet
> Ou l'estrivet capiel donnet.
> (*Li Méditations,* in *Poésies,* 1:89, ll. 16–17)

> [In the *puys* he was crowned, where he was given the contended wreath.]

At the beginning of *Li Regret Guillaume, comte de Hainaut,* Jean de Le Mote states that he dreams of taking one of his love songs to a *puy* and of winning the crown:

> Dis k'à .i. puis le porteroie
> Pour couronner, se je pooie   (Ll. 103–4)

The *chansons royales* of Jean Froissart were crowned at Valenciennes, Abbeville, Lille, and Tournai. We need to look more closely at this artistic sovereignty in the territories from Tournai to Avignon —a sovereignty that had no political meaning and was, in all cases, purely poetic. One sure guide is Dom Jean Leclercq's excellent book on monastic literature in the twelfth century, *L'Amour des lettres et le désir de Dieu* (*The Love of Learning and the Desire for God*), first published in 1947.

By the fourteenth century, writers were no longer uniquely in the monastic environment; thus we need to listen for vernacular French, which was by then becoming well established, seeking its own character in relation to Latin and to the other vulgar tongues that were emerging as national languages. A love of letters—Latin letters—had by then become a love of books. The book was coming to be appreciated as an object, and the century was turning bibliophile. The desire for God passed also through personal desires.

The literature of the fourteenth century operated at a "second degree" in a conscious effort to rewrite earlier books. It devoted lively, insistent, penetrating, and often anxious reflection to "coming after." What did it mean for men of that time to work under an overwhelming feeling that they came—and were—"second"?

Medieval literature was created in French between the ninth and the twelfth centuries. Even though from the long-term perspective the fourteenth century seems still quite close to the point of origin of vernacular French, the poets of the time—precisely because of that proximity—thought of themselves as sons of their forebears, but sons who moved in a world grown old. They found the contradiction painful; it gave their literature a color of its own—the color of melancholy. There had been a springtime of literature in the twelfth century, a time of joyous exaltation and of pioneers, when everything had to be reinvented in French. The fourteenth century, in contrast, saw itself as the winter of literature, a time of retreat into one's self and of enclosure, reflection, and old age. This is what Johan Huizinga so admirably depicted in his *The Autumn of the Middle Ages.* We need to reflect on the aesthetic, philosophic, and affective reasons that lead us, today, to turn once again to that period. A world we see as young felt itself to be old. It saw itself as the last age of humanity, and it found signs that Judgment was nigh:

> Les signes voy que li cours muera
> De ce monde qui approuche sa fin.
>> (Eustache Deschamps, *Oeuvres complètes,*
>> 1:142, no. 52, ll. 5–6)

[I see the signs that foretell that the course of this world, which approaches its end, will change.]

The triumphant twelfth century had stated, in Latin, "We are dwarfs perched on the shoulders of giants. Hence we see more and farther than they." We owe this superb image to Bernard of Chartres, a great teacher of the first third of the twelfth century; it was repeated by John of Salisbury in his *Metalogicon,* written around 1159. The image expresses both an essential humility ("we are dwarfs") and an optimism about knowledge that found an echo in the vernacular literature of the time. In the prologue to her *Lais,* Marie de France writes:

> Li philosophe le saveient,
> Par eux meïsmes entendeient,
> Cum plus trespassereit li tens,
> Plus serreient sutil de sens
> E plus se savraient garder
> De ceo k'i ert a trespasser   (Ll. 17–22)

[The philosophers knew this; they understood by themselves that the more that time passed, the more subtle men's minds would be and the more care they would take about what they interpreted.]

We need to set Marie's optimism and her belief in progress against the rondeau of Charles d'Orléans entitled "Escollier de Merencolye" (Melancholy's pupil). Here the poet feels himself a "wrinkled child" who has become an old man ("vieillart devenu") and is forced to study under Melancholy's rule:

> Escollier de Merencolye,
> Des verges de Soussy batu,
> Je suis a l'estude tenu,
> Es derreniers jours de ma vye.
>
> (*Poésies,* vol. 2, rondeau 397)

> [Pupil of Melancholy, beaten with the switches of Care, I am put to «its» study in the last days of my life.]

An age trapped in contradiction, peopled with aging sons and old schoolchildren, displayed a painful tension.

2 ▮ *At Wits' End*

Losing One's Latin

We can find the schoolboy "beaten with switches"—the switches of grammar this time, not of care—on cathedral portals, in particular, of the Cathedral of Chartres. *Grammar* meant Latin; it was the first of the arts of the *trivium*—the basis of medieval schooling—and it was a requirement for subsequent study of logic, dialectic, and rhetoric. Latin was the language of unity and of authority: the unity of a Europe of clerics, the authority of the church in its religious teaching and of knowledge in general. Where was the French language on that map, and what advantages could it offer?

Writing in French was by no means a novelty in the fourteenth century, but it remained a choice involving cultural values. French was gaining ground in domains that had been the exclusive province of Latin, and it was beginning to have a political impact. It was thought of as a language of culture: in England, for example, it was studied on a par with Latin. The manuals that taught French, as a mother would teach her child, were called *feminae*. "Liber iste vocatur femina quia sicut femina docet infantem loqui maternam sic docet iste liber iuvenes rethorice loqui Gallicum" (*Femina,* 28) [This book is called *femina* because, just as the woman teaches the child his native tongue, so does this book teach children to speak French well].

In England, the French language reflected both terms of the Latin/ vernacular dichotomy in that it was undeniably a learned language— learned by the book—but that book played a motherly role.

French was also put to the test as the stakes and the instrument of power. Within France that process began in 1274, when the memoirs of the royal dynasties, the *Chronicles of Saint-Denis* (originally written in Latin) were translated into French under the title *Grandes Chroniques de France* and, after 1340, were written directly in French. A transfer of knowledge went hand in hand with transfer of power. Outside the kingdom of France, one of the arguments put forth by the king of England in support of his claim to the French throne in the dispute regarding the succession of Philip IV (Philippe le Bel) was his mastery of the French language. But if the French language provided the English king with an argument in favor of his dynastic claims in the power struggle between France and England, within France it became a means to power and an instrument of the political program of Charles V, "the Wise."

An Unlettered King Is Like an Ass with a Crown

Wisdom was a royal virtue par excellence. The Bible said so (the usual reference was to Solomon), and the notion was never contested during the Middle Ages. What is interesting to examine is how, beginning in the twelfth century, wisdom—*sagesse*—gradually changed into a knowledge—*sapience*—that it was the prince's duty to acquire. Taking as a point of departure John of Salisbury's maxim in his *Policraticus* (4.6), "Rex illiteratus quasi asinus coronatus," we need to examine the fortunes of this image in French during the fourteenth century. John's *Policraticus* was translated into French in 1372, at the command of Charles V, by Denis Foulechat, a Franciscan friar. The passage runs thus in French: "Je me recorde que es letres que le roy des Romains escript au roy de France je treuve en l'une entre les autres, où il amonnestoit et conseilloit que il feist ses enfanz aprendre es ars liberaulz et en bonnes doctrines, que il disoit que roy qui n'est lettré est comme asne coroné" (*Policraticus*, bk. 4, chap. 6, p. 65) [I

7

remember that in the letters that the king of the Romans «Conrad III» wrote to the king of France «Louis VII», I found one, among others, in which he encouraged him and advised him to have his children taught the liberal arts and right doctrines, for he said that a king who is unlettered is like a crowned ass].

In *Le Songe du vergier,* another work written (in 1376) at the command of Charles V, first in Latin and then in French, the knight, after insisting at length on the need for a "lettered" king, states: "Un Roy sanz lattreüre est conme une nef sanz avyrons, et come oysel sanz elles" (bk. 1, chap. 132, sec. 5, p. 223) [A king without letters is like a boat without oars, and like a bird without wings].

Eustache Deschamps (1346–1406) spelled out in a ballade what the king's program of studies should be:

> Roy sans lettres comme un asne seroit
> S'il ne sçavoit l'escripture ou les loys,
> Chascun de ly par tout se moqueroit;
> Thiès doivent savoir, latin, françoys.
> > (*Oeuvres complètes,* 5:255–56, no. 1001, ll. 17–20)

[A king without letters would be like an ass if he did not know the Holy Scriptures and the laws; everywhere, everyone would make fun of him; kings must know German, Latin, French.]

Eustache Deschamps returned to that advice in the refrain of another ballade: "Roy sanz lettre est comme asne couronné" (6:254–56, no. 1244).

Christine de Pizan punctuated her lessons to princes with the same idea: "Roy sans clergie est asne couronné." In her *Livre du chemin de long estude,* she returned to the passage in Denis Foulechat's translation of John of Salisbury and amplified it:

> On treuve en histoires de France
> Comment en lettres de creance
> Le roy des Rommains une fois
> Si escripst au roy des François.   (Ll. 5075–78)

[One finds in the histories of France how, in a diplomatic
letter of accreditation, the king of the Romans once wrote
to the king of the French.]

Christine ends her exemplum thus:

> Puis conclut que roy non savant
> Tout son fait n'estoit que droit vent,
> Et d'autant valoit au regné
> Com feist un asne couronné.   (Ll. 5089–92)

[Then he concluded that all the exploits of an ignorant king
were but wind, and that he would count as much in the
kingdom as a crowned ass.]

By its forceful interplay of opposites and by the eloquence of its
image, the aphorism captured the political thought of the epoch. It
figured in the introductions to most documents transferring *auctoritates.* Knowledge, which enabled the sovereign to avoid tyranny, was
necessary to the exercise of governmental functions. Kingdoms
would not last without it. Christine de Pizan put that opinion into
the mouth of Charles V, her model of the wise king, in *Le Livre des
fais et bonnes meurs* (bk. 3, chap. 14, p. 49), and the thought persisted
over the centuries. In 1776, Baron d'Holbach cited Christine's book
in his *Ethocratie,* written in support of Turgot. In the fourteenth century, we can find the same statement in identical form in the *Livre de
Ethiques d'Aristote* of Nicole Oresme (p. 99) and in the *Archiloge Sophie* of Jacques Legrand (bk. 1, chap. 7, p. 43).

Knowledge had a political role to play, and Charles V initiated a
veritable language policy by commissioning a considerable number of
translations and by organizing the royal library of the Louvre, which
Christine de Pizan (*Livre des fais,* bk. 3, chap. 12, p. 42) called a "belle
assemblée des notables livres et belle librarie" [fine collection of important books and . . . great library (Willard translation, 240)].

Translation as Choice

One practical result of this move to produce translations was that Latin no longer enjoyed quite such a sacred relation to knowledge. Early in the fourteenth century, in Cysoing, near Lille, an anonymous Dominican translated into French the *Ludus super Anticlaudianum* of Adam de la Bassée (a canon of the Lille cathedral who had died in 1286). The translator felt a lingering need to justify his enterprise, and he did so in the name of the principle of diversity: just as one could appreciate roses of different colors, white and red wine, white and black bread, and variety in horses' gaits (trot, gallop, walk), one could also savor an aphorism from a work regardless of the language in which it was written: "En quel langue qu'elle soit mise" (prologue, l. 33).

> Et pour chou ay m'entente mise
> A un poete translater
> En roumant, pour men tamps passer.[1]   (Ll. 34–36)

[That is why I have occupied my time translating a *poète* «i.e., an authority» into the vernacular.]

Nicole Oresme, Charles V's great translator, developed the theme in his *Livre de Ethiques d'Aristote.* Oresme placed Latin in historical perspective, asserting that Latin had been to Greek what the French language now was to Latin. In other words, Latin, the language of authority, of the symbolic *father,* had been the *mother* tongue of the ancient Romans: "Et en ce pays, le langage commun et maternel c'estoit latin" (101). Up to that date, Latin and French had been seen in hierarchical terms, a convention that was at times bolstered by the use of categories borrowed from the feudal vocabulary: "Lo latino è sovrano del volgare" [Latin is the sovereign of the vernacular (Lansing translation, 17)], Dante declared in his *Convivio* (1:7). Today, we analyze the relationship between Latin and the vernacular languages in terms of chronological succession. In that age, a historical vision was gaining ground over the theological vision, although at times

---

1. Transcription by Marc-René Jung, *Etudes sur le poème allégorique en France au Moyen Age,* 99.

scholars confronted with the desacralization of Latin put up a symptomatic resistance. In Florence, Leonardo Bruni (1370–1444) argued in his letters, as Michael Baxandall reminds us in his *Giotto and the Orators*, that "the common people of ancient Rome could not have managed the difficulties of Latin: what they had spoken was a sort of Italian, and Latin had been an élite culture language" (2).

In the last analysis, reflection on language became reflection on history. There are some interesting examples of this. In his *Sermon sur la Passion,* preached before King Charles VI, Jean Courtecuisse (who was bishop of Geneva when he died in 1423) displayed a sensitivity to the language spoken by Christ's disciples. Quoting the servant woman who upbraided Peter and adding a remark of his own, he states: "'Vraiement tu en est! La parolle t'accuse; il appert bien que tu es de Galilée.' Tous parloient ebrieu, mais avait entre eulz difference comme entre françois et picart" (sec. 45, p. 66) ["Truly, you are one of them! Your speech betrays you; it is easy to tell that you are from Galilee." Everyone was speaking Hebrew, but with differences among them as between French and Picard].

Jacques de Bugnin, who was born in Lausanne, noted in his *Congié pris du siecle seculier,* a work he completed in the monastery of Tamié, in Savoy, on 3 July 1480, that his native language was not French but Savoyard:

> Car du dicteur la langue nutritive
> Partit premier du pays de Savoye.   (Ll. 49–50)

> [For the author's nurturing language came first from the land of Savoy.]

Langue nutritive is an expression worth noting. According to the dual meaning of the verb *nourrir* in Old French, Savoyard nourished him and instructed him, like mother's milk and the mother's speech.

Anyone Who Does Not Go Abroad Knows Nothing

These first signs of a looser attachment to Latin permitted the age to become interested in other languages. Differences among languages were perceived, noted, and commented on, a change that may reflect a new way of getting about in the world and a new sensitivity to the speech of the lands that a traveler visited. Even in the domain of fiction the mention of language could recreate travel impressions. Thus Jean Froissart notes that his hero, Meliador, the son of the duke of Cornwall, sings a rondeau "en Breton, non pas en françois" [in Breton, not in French] as he rides through the Northumberland countryside (*Meliador,* vol. 1, l. 7741). The rondeau that follows is in French. Eustache Deschamps complained of having to travel in Germany and in Bohemia, where, among the many other trials he had to endure (uncomfortable lodgings, filth, execrable food, the natives' deplorable table manners), there were "les langaiges qu'om n'entent pas" (*Oeuvres complètes,* 7:69, no. 1311, l. 7) [the languages one doesn't understand]:

> Je suis aux abais comme uns cerfs,
> Et n'entens chose qu'om me die
> En aleman, for entre clers
> Le latin. Or ne treuve mie
> Tousjours clers; s'ay trop dure vie,
> Car la nature d'Alemans
> Est, ou ilz scevent bien roumans,
> Puis qu'il y ait un seul François,
> Si demourrait entr'eul XX ans,
> Ja n'y parleront que thioys.   (7:61, no. 1305, ll. 1–10)

> [I am at bay like a stag and understand nothing that is said to me in German. All I understand is the clerics' Latin. But I do not always meet clerics. The life I lead is truly too harsh, for it is typical of the Germans that even if they know French, since there is but one Frenchman, and even if he were to live among them twenty years, they would still speak only German.]

This did not stop Eustache Deschamps from concluding that travel was a necessary and formative experience: "Il ne scet rien qui ne va hors" [He who does not go abroad knows nothing], as he states in the refrain to the ballade (no. 1311). Before him, Guillaume de Machaut, who was secretary to the king of Bohemia, Jean de Luxembourg, and accompanied the king in his travels, had similar difficulties:

> Car le païs m'estoit sauvage,
> Et ne savoie le langage.
> (*Le Dit de la Fonteinne amoureuse,* in
Oeuvres, 3:148, ll. 149–50)

[The country moreover was unfamiliar to me, and I couldn't speak the language (Palmer translation, 97).]

People began to reflect on what it meant to learn a language, and they began to think in terms of comparing languages. In his *Paradis de la reine Sibylle,* Antoine de La Sale (1386–ca. 1461), a squire in the service of the dukes of Anjou and a great traveler, pointed out that it was one thing to be able to understand a language and quite another to be able to speak it. The inhabitants of his paradise—a marvelous kingdom and an inverted Christian Paradise—had the gift of tongues. Their ability to speak languages was acquired according to a chronology unique to that other-worldly kingdom: "Car celle royne et toutes celles et ceulx de leans scevent parler tous les languaiges du monde dès aussi tost qu'ilz ont leans esté par l'espace de IIIᶜXXX jours; et depuis que un y est et a passé IX jours, il les entent trestous ainsi que le sien proprement, mais n'en sçaura parler mot de nul, jusques au terme passé, que ceulx qu'il scet" (*La Salade,* 93) [For that queen and all the ladies and gentlemen from there know all languages in the world from the moment they have been there three hundred thirty days; and as soon as anyone finds himself there and has spent nine days there, he understands all languages as well as his own, but he cannot speak a word of any of them, aside from those he knows, before the end of that period].

Antoine de La Sale was also interested in comparing languages. He reports his interlocutor's reply to his inquiry about the geographical origins of some visitors to this paradise: "Mais, selon son advis, devoit estre des parties de Gascongne ou de Languedoc; car lui et le plus de ses gens disoient *oc,* le languaige que l'en parle quant l'en vait a Saint Jacques. Autres enseignes ne m'en sceut a dire" (122) [But in his opinion, he must be from the region of Gascony or Languedoc, for he and most of his men spoke *oc,* the language spoken when one goes to St. James of Compostela. He could give me no further information].

In poetry, diversity among languages became a metaphor for other complexities. The little circle around Charles d'Orléans at Blois in the mid-fifteenth century exercised its wit on the notion of the *truchement,* or interpreter, written *trichement* in some manuscripts that used paronomasia to bend the word into trickery. The old play on the words *traduire/trahir* (translate/betray) had a number of variations. Charles d'Orléans wrote:

> Le trucheman de ma pensee,
> Qui parle maint divers langaige,
> M'a rapporté chose sauvaige
> Que je n'ay point acoustumee.
>
> En françoys la m'a translatee,
> Comme tressouffisant et saige,
> Le trucheman [de ma pensee,
> Que parle maint divers langaige].
>
> Quant mon cueur l'a bien escoutee,
> Il lui a dit: Vous faittes raige,
> Oncques mais n'ouy tel messaige;
> Venez vous d'estrange contree,
> Le trucheman [de ma pensee]?   (Vol. 2, rondeau 211)

[The interpreter of my thought, who speaks many different languages, brought me back a strange thing totally unfamiliar to me. He translated it into French for me, like an accomplished and competent person, the interpreter of my thought, who speaks many different languages. After having listened well to him, my heart told him: You are mad; I have never heard such a message. Do you come from a foreign land, interpreter of my thought?]

Charles d'Orléans ended another rondeau thus:

> Et qui n'a pas langaige en lui
> Pour parler selon son désir,

Ung truchement lui fault querir;
Ainsi, ou par la ou par cy,
A trompeur [trompeur et demi].   (Vol. 2, rondeau 163)

[And anyone who does not himself possess a language for
speaking as he wishes must seek out an interpreter; and so,
in one way or another, for the trickster there's a trickster and
a half.]

People of the late Middle Ages drew pleasure from this diversity,
whether they found it charming or were somewhat repulsed by it.
They also found profit in it. Etienne de Conty (d. 1413), an *official*
(judge in an ecclesiastical court) from Corbie, added to a list in his
Brevis tractatus of the advantages of his homeland the three languages
most commonly spoken there: *gallicus, flamingus, britonicus.* Languages gave pleasure because they provided a relationship experienced in aesthetic terms as beauty, ugliness, or sensuality. French was
doux (sweet, gentle): a conversation manual composed in England in
1396, *La Manière de langage qui enseigne à bien parler et écrire le
français,* promised to teach a "doulz françois selon l'usage et la coustume de France" [gentle French according to the usage and custom of
France]. French was so soft to the ears that its beauty and sweetness
could be compared "au parler des angels du ciel, pour la grand doul-
ceur et biaultee d'icel" [to the speech of the angels in heaven, for its
great softness and beauty].

This *doux français*—this "sweetest" idiom, as Dante called it—
that absorbed different dialects was the very stuff of literature: it was
the *douceur* of the mother; *douceur* of France, the France of dreams;
the *dulce France* of *La Chanson de Roland.* John Barton promised in
his *Donait françois*—a *Donat,* or grammar, written about 1400—that
he would introduce his readers to the "droit language du Paris et de
pais la d'entour, la quelle language in Engliterre on appelle: doulce
France" [genuine language of Paris and the surrounding territories,
which in England is called "sweet France"].

Latin, on the other hand, was forceful. A variant of the prologue
of the Cysoing Dominican's translation of Adam de la Bassée's *Ludus*

super Anticlaudianum replaces "un poete translater" with the phrase,
"j. [un] fort livre translater"—that is, a book in Latin. Christine de
Pizan reverentially insists on Charles V's command of Latin: "mais
non obstant que bien entendist le latin et que ja ne fust besoing que
on lui exposast" (*Le Livre des fais et des bonnes meurs du sage roy
Charles V,* bk. 3, chap. 12, pp. 42–43) [even though he understood
Latin well and there was no need of translating for him (Willard
translation, 240)]. Still, she admits: "Pour ce que peut-estre n'avoit le
latin, pour la *force* [emphasis added] des termes soubtilz, si en usage
comme la lengue françoise, fist de theologie translater plusieurs livres
de saint Augustin" (bk. 3, chap. 3, p. 13) [Because he may not have
had sufficient Latin for such subtle matters that are more commonly
explained in Latin than in French, he had translated several books on
theology by Saint Augustine (Willard translation, 240)].

This strong, forceful Latin—Simon de Hesdin, the commander
of the house of the Hospitalers of St. John of Jerusalem of Eterpigny
(in Picardy) who translated Valerius Maximus for Charles V around
1375, called it a dense, difficult language—had its nostalgic admirers.
Philippe de Mézières recommended to Charles VI, through the
mouth of Vérité (Truth) in *Le Songe du vieil pelerin,* completed in
1389, that he read Latin as much as possible, the Bible in particular:

Et soies certains que se tu te delicteras a lire le latin, une hystoire
ou enseignemens te plairont mieulx au cuer que dimie dozeime
d'ystoires en françoys. Car la saincte escripture, escripte et dictee
par les sains en latin et depuis translatee en françois, ne rent pas
telle substance aux lisans, es ruisseaux, comme elle fait en sa propre fontayne. Quel merveille! car il y a en la sainte escripture certains et plusieurs motz en latin qui du lisant percent le cuer en
grant devocion, lesquelx translatez en françois se treuvent en vul-
gal sans saveur et sans delectacion.   (2:223–24)

[And be assured that if you take pleasure in reading Latin, a history or a lesson will please your heart better than a half-dozen histories in French. For Holy Writ, written and composed by the
saints in Latin and since translated into French, does not give the
same substance to those who read it in its streams as it does when

read at its very source. What a marvel! for there are in Holy Writ many words that pierce the reader's heart through with a great devotion, words that, once translated into French, are in the vulgar tongue without savor and without delight.]

Language, be it Latin or French, was also a source of pleasure. As for knowledge, some people in the fourteenth century lost more than their Latin. Gilles Li Muisis tells us twice in his *Poésies* (1:222, l. 6; 1:357, l. 11), "Je pierc men walesc"—"I'm wasting my time."

3 The Genealogy Hunt

At the opening of *Le Plait de l'evesque et de droit,* Jean Le Court, called Brisebare, who came from Douai, reflected on a statement he attributed to "Caton le Sage" (Cato the Elder):

> Biaus fis,
> va as plais et as parlemens
> pour aprendre les jugemens. (Ll. 4–6)

> [Dear son, go to the law courts and the audience halls to hear the decisions.]

He hesitated over the term of address but decided that one could indeed hold Cato to be a father:

> puis c'om poet pour voir maintenir
> qu'il poet bien plus d'un peres iestre:
> nous avons Dieu, le roi celiestre,
> a Pere par creation;
> peres d'autre condition,
> si c'Adans fu et Abrehans,
> pere anciien par plenté d'ans;
> or s'avons no pere carnel,
> et no pere spirituel
> —c'est papes, prelas u curés—

dont mains cuers est souvent curés;
et s'avons pere par doctrinne.   (Ll. 10–21)

[since in truth one can state that more than one father can
exist at one time: we have God, the heavenly King, for Father by creation; we have fathers of another sort, father patriarchs such as Adam and Abraham; we have our father of
the flesh and our spiritual father—the pope, the prelates,
and parish priests—by whom many hearts are often puri-
fied; and we have a father in studies.]

The multiplicity of fathers raised questions of authority and submission. How could these different allegiances be reconciled? And
what was the sons' place?

The Names of God

We read in the epilogue to the *Avionnet,* the work of a compiler
from Burgundy who was offering the fables he had collected (some
time between 1339 and 1348) to Jeanne de Bourgogne, the wife of
Philip VI:

Toute science vient du Pere
De lumiere, de ce me pere.
                    (*Recueil général des Isopets,* 2:382, ll. 25–26)

[All knowledge comes from the Father of light, that is clear
to me.]

This was the usual position of reverence and submission: all
knowledge came from God and—as we note with interest in this
mid-fourteenth century—from a God who is Father. Historians of
art tell us that only with the fourteenth century was the figure of God
the Father represented as distinct from that of Christ. The figure of
God the Father crystallized around the description in Daniel (7.9–13)
of the Ancient of Days. A comparison of the designations of God in
a twelfth-century mystery play, *Le Jeu d'Adam,* and in a fifteenth-century text, Arnoul Gréban's *Le Mystère de la Passion,* confirm the nov-

---

elty of the figure. In the 944 verse lines of the *Jeu d'Adam,* God, in relation to his creatures, is designated as *createur* (in 11 instances), *dampnedeu* (1), *roi* (3), and *sire* or *seigneur* (19). In the first "day" of the *Mystère de la Passion* (9,943 verse lines), we find: *acteur* (2), *createur* (11), *creeur* (2), *firmateur* (1), *gouvernement* (1), *juge* (24, 18 of them in *Le Procès de justice et de miséricorde*), *pere* (12), *plasmateur* (2), *principe* (1), *roi* (7), *sire* (8), and *souverain* (1).

While the terms *createur, roi,* and *sire* or *seigneur* are common to the two texts, the term *pere* appears only in the second. Its appearance, along with its frequency (a higher number of instances than for the word *createur*), indicates a new sensibility and an affective perception of the relationship of God to his creatures. This relationship was thought of more in terms of filiation, of genealogy, than in feudal terms. We might also note the decline in frequency of the word *sire* to designate God the Father, as well as the use of the word *dampnedeu—Dominus Deus, Seigneur Dieu,* or Lord God—exclusively in *Le Jeu d'Adam.* The question of the father—or of fathers—was on the agenda of the age. There were other fathers in the spiritual domain—the church fathers for matters of doctrine and, especially, the popes, "no Sains-Pères" (our Holy Fathers), as Gilles Li Muisis calls them, tracing their history in his own day, beginning with Pope Celestine V: "Car des autres devant ne saroie-jou parler, pour chou que jou estoie uns jovenechiaus et pensoie pau à tels coses" (1:299) [For of those who preceded him I cannot speak, because I was a young man and thought little of such things].

The question of spiritual fathers was complicated in the fourteenth century by the schism in the church. To have more than one pope at a given time was a sign of excess and error. Eustache Deschamps said as much with vigor:

> O bilinguis, qui trovas tel cautelle,
> Trop fus emflez de malice et d'orgueil,
> Et le clergié fut de legier acueil,
> En ce faisant; casser le voy et croistre
> Comme la noix, ou l'escaille d'une oistre.
> *(Oeuvres complètes,* 6:192–93, no. 1204, ll. 29–33)

[O double-tongued man, who found such a ruse! You were too swollen with malice and pride, and the clergy was thoughtless to welcome such a thing; I see it breaking and shattering like a walnut or an oyster shell.]

To have two popes was to have no authentic pope. Eustache Deschamps punctuated his ballade with the refrain, "Vray pappe n'es n'empereur en l'Eglise" [There is no true pope nor emperor in the church]. An abundance of fathers, with no hierarchical order among them, was harmful.

Fathers and Sons: From King to King with the Knights

The same abundance of fathers tainted historical genealogies as well. Criticizing the way in which Bartholomaeus Anglicus viewed the history of England in his *De proprietatibus rerum,* written between 1240 and 1260, Jean Corbechon, who translated the work into French at the command of Charles V between 1369 and 1372, stated: "Secondement, il cuide louer ce pays et il le blasme, car il dit que ilz descendirent en premier des geans, et puis de Brut et de ceulx de Troye la Grant, et puis des Saxons. En disant ainsi, il les fait bastars en leur donnant plusieurs peres" (*Le Livre des proprietez des choses,* fol. 230c–d) [Second, he thinks to praise that country but he speaks ill of it, for he says first that they descended from the giants, and then from Brutus and the Trojans, and then from the Saxons. So saying he makes them bastards by giving them several fathers].

Above all, Jean Corbechon found it reprehensible to boast about several successive invasions (that was where the bastardy came in) but to forget the one that carried the most prestige in French eyes—the Norman conquest:

> Et ce ne fait pas a oublier, car moins de honte leur est de estre conquis par les Francoys ou par les Northmans que d'estre conquis par les Saxons; si deüst avoir eu toutes ces conquestes laissees pour couvrir leur honte; ou s'il le tient a honneur, il ne devoit pas oublier la conqueste du duc Guillaume dont le roy des Angloys porte les armes, avec un peu d'ajoustement. (Ibid.)

[And that should not be forgotten, for there is for them less shame in having been conquered by the French or by the Normans than in having been conquered by the Saxons; he should have left out all those conquests to hide his country's shame; or, if he holds «conquest» for an honor, he should not forget the conquest of Duke William, whose arms, with some slight adjustment, are worn by the English people's king.]

Thus, for a partisan observer like Jean Corbechon, the English were bastards, while the French line, which went back to a demigod, was pure. He added a passage developing Bartholomeus Anglicus's very brief remarks on the origin of the French:

Les autres, qui ont plus veü des Croniques de France, dient que France est ainsi appellee de Francion, le filz de Hercules et nepveu du roy Priant, lequel Francion aprés la destruccion de Troyes la Grant se parti de son pays a grant compaignie de nobles gens de son lignage et d'autre, et vint par deça. Et de son nom fut appellee France, si comme dient maistre Hue de Saint Victor et maistre Hue de Cligny et plusieurs autres authentiques croniqueres.

(Fol. 237c)

[Others, who have examined the Chronicles of France in greater depth, say that France takes its name from Francion, the son of Hercules «in fact, Hector» and nephew «grandson» of King Priam. That Francion, after the destruction of Great Troy, left his country with a large company of nobles of his lineage and other lineages and came to these parts. And France was called by his name, as is told by Master Hugh of St. Victor and Master Hugh of Cluny and several other truthful chroniclers.]

Historical fathers, remote fathers, temporal fathers: for religious and cultural reasons, paternity was a model in the thought of the Middle Ages. This means that we need to be aware of the father-and-son pairs who occupied the political and literary arenas of the fourteenth century, beginning with the princes, great lords, and kings of France.

There is one time-honored legend, one image of a royal father and his sons that history books for children have imprinted on French minds, that of King John II—Jean le Bon—and his sons at the bat-

tle of Poitiers (1356). Michelet makes a superb scene of it. We all have
in our ears the "Father, watch out to the right! Watch out to the left!"
[Padre, guardatevi a destra o a sinistra] (*Cronica,* bk. 7, chap. 19, p.
22)) that Matteo Villani, who continued the *Chronicle* of his brother
Giovanni, attributes to fourteen-year-old Philippe, Jean le Bon's
youngest son. Legend has it that Philippe's bravery in that battle won
him the sobriquet "le Hardi" (the Bold) and the duchy of Burgundy.
The king's other three sons had been sent away from the battlefield at
the king's command. Because he was not present at the final moment
of the combat, and because of his father's subsequent capitivity in
England, the dauphin, the future Charles V, was deprived of his
chance to be a son. He had to govern (and he did govern) not under
the sign of youth but under that of old age. As Jules Michelet put it,
"Le jeune roi était né vieux" [The young king was born old]. He was
in harmony with his century. According to Christine de Pizan,
Charles died a patriarch's death: "En approchant le terme de la fin, en
la maniere des Peres patriarches du viel Testament, fist amener devant
lui son filz ainsné, le dauphin" (*Le Livre des fais et bonnes meurs,*
2:190) [While approaching the time of his end, in the manner of the
ancient patriarchs of the Old Testament, he had his oldest son, the
dauphin, led before him (Willard translation, 245)].

This happened in 1380. The king was forty-two years old. If
Charles V had neither the time nor the inclination to be a son, his
own son would never be anything but. The paternal image left by
Charles V was a heavy burden to bear, and insanity (discernible as
early as 1392, when Charles VI was twenty-four) kept the young king
in an eternal infancy and a perpetual dependency.

Another important royal pair was Jean de Luxembourg, "le bon
roi de Behaingne" [the good king of Bohemia], Charles V's maternal
grandfather, and the son born of his second marriage, Wenceslas of
Brabant. Writers of the fourteenth century depicted both men as exemplary patrons. From about 1323, when he entered the king's service, Guillaume de Machaut served Jean de Luxembourg as *clerc au-
monier, notaire,* and then *secrétaire.* Recalling those years in *La Prise
d'Alexandrie,* Guillaume proclaimed proudly:

> Je fu ses clers, ans plus de XXX,
> Si congnu ses meurs et s'entente,
> S'onneur, son bien, sa gentillesse,
> Son hardement et sa largesse,
> Car j'estoie ses secretaires
> En trestous ses plus gros affaires.   (Ll. 785–90)

[I was his clerk for more than thirty years. I knew his ways and his thoughts, his honor, his wealth, his nobility, his bravery, and his generosity, for I was his secretary in all his most important affairs.]

Guillaume accompanied the king through all his voyages and expeditions, which means that he traveled throughout Europe. His writings bear warm and frequent witness to his admiration for King John. The king is the central figure in *Le Jugement dou roy de Behaingne,* and Guillaume holds him up as a model for Charles de Navarre in *Le Confort d'Ami.* John appears again in *La Fonteinne amoureuse* and in *La Prise d'Alexandrie.* Guillaume praises his valor and his liberality, both eminently chivalric qualities:

> Il donnoit fiez, joiaus et terre,
> Or, argent; riens ne retenoit
> Fors l'onneur.
>   (*Le Confort d'Ami,* in *Oeuvres,* vol. 3, ll. 2930–32)

[He gave away fiefs, jewels, land, gold, and silver; he kept back nothing but honor.]

Jean de Luxembourg died on the battlefield at Crécy in 1346 in a heroic and theatrical manner: by then blind, he threw himself into the fray, his horse attached to those of Henri Le Moine de Bâle and Henri de Klingenberg, two of his knights. Writers saw this death as marking the end of an era. Jean Froissart recalled it in 1372 in *La Prison amoureuse.* Jean de Luxembourg had managed to use an infirmity that was considered traumatizing and degrading in the Middle Ages and make it the emblem of his courage—a *blind* courage. He became the ideal prince, the last of an extinct race. Later writers looked back nostalgically to the happier days of the good king of Bohemia. Eustache Deschamps, in *Le Lay de plour,* stressed his valor:

Au temps de ce vaillant Roy
Joustes, festes et tournoy
Et toute vie joyeuse
Estoient en grant arroy,
Amour, deduit, esbanoy
Et toute loy amoureuse;
Vaillance estoit vertueuse,
Nul n'osast faire desroy.
Helas! autrement perçoy
La chose trop perilleuse.

    (*Oeuvres complètes*, 2:312–13, no. 310, ll. 197–206)

[In the days of that valiant king, jousts, festivities, tournaments, and all sorts of joyous life were honored «along
with» love, pleasure, amusements, and all loving law; valor
was virtuous, no one would have dared stray from the right
path. Alas, I see things otherwise, as most perilous.]

Jean Froissart, who knew John of Bohemia (Jean de Luxembourg)
only through Machaut (Froissart calls him "Karle, le roi de Behagne,"
mistaking him for his eldest son, Charles), cites him as an example of
liberality at the beginning of *La Prison amoureuse*: "qui faire a tous
largece ensagne" [who teaches all to practice largesse]. Froissart then
elaborates:

Li bons rois que je nomme chi,
C'est chils qui remest a Crechi,
Qui tant fu larges et courtois
Que, de Prusse jusqu'en Artois,
Non, jusques en Constantinnoble,
N'i eut plus large ne plus noble.   (Ll. 65–70)

[The good king whom I name here is the one who died at
Crécy, who was so generous and so courteous that, from
Prussia to Artois—no, to Constantinople—there was no
one more generous or more noble than he.]

Jean de Luxembourg was a *preux*—a valiant, "worthy" knight—a
new Alexander and a new Hector. This is how Guillaume de
Machaut presents him in *Le Jugement dou roy de Behaingne*, suggesting him as someone capable of judging the debate,

car de largesse
Passe Alixandre et Hector de prouesse.

(*Oeuvres,* vol. 1, ll. 1296–97)

[since in generosity he surpasses Alexander, and Hector in prowess (Palmer translation, 57).]

The idealized figure of Jean de Luxembourg continued throughout the fourteenth century to serve as a nostalgic reference point and model. It was a sign of the times that the nostalgia began to operate almost immediately.

Jean de Luxembourg's eldest son, Charles, who became Holy Roman Emperor as Charles IV, was a writer. He wrote his autobiography, the *Vita Karoli,* in Latin. Petrarch admired him and in the early 1350s invited him to come make his imperial residence in Rome. Wenceslas of Brabant, Jean's son by his second wife, was a poet, according to Wenceslas's protégé, Jean Froissart, who depicted the son with as much enthusiasm as he had the father. Froissart states in *Le Dit dou florin,*

Car uns princes fu amourous,
Gracious et chevalerous

("*Dits*" et "*Débats,*" 184, ll. 305–6)

[For he was a loving, gracious, and chivalrous prince]

and in the *Chroniques,* "En ce temps trespassa de cest siècle, en la duchié de Lucembourcq, li jolis et gentils duc Wincelins de Boesme, dus de Lucembourch et de Braibant, qui fu en son temps nobles, jolis, frisques, sages, armerès et amoureux" (2:155) [At that time there disappeared from the world in the duchy of Luxembourg the gay and well-born Duke Wenceslas of Bohemia, duke of Luxembourg and of Brabant, who was in his life noble, handsome, lively, wise, valiant, and amorous (translation based on Jolliffe translation, 262)]. Wenceslas came to a less glorious end than Jean de Luxembourg, however: he died of leprosy in 1383.

A third princely father and son duo, Gaston Phoebus, the count of Foix, and his son Gaston, intrigued chroniclers and men of letters for the drama that occurred between them when the count killed his only legitimate son. It was before Gaston Phoebus that Jean Froissart read his *Meliador,* a romance into which he introduced the lyric poetry of Wenceslas of Brabant. Phoebus was a writer too, the author of a famous treatise on hunting. The drama is magnificently told by Jean Froissart. As he traveled through Béarn, Froissart tells us, he persistently sought information about the mysterious death of young Gaston. His traveling companion, Espang de Lyon, refused to tell him anything about it, but Froissart finally got the story from "ung escuier ancien et homme moult notable" (*Chroniques,* 12:79) [an old and important squire (Jolliffe translation, 284)] whose name he does not give. Gaston Phoebus's legitimate heir bled to death in 1380 when his hunter father, perhaps inadvertently, slit his jugular vein after imprisoning the young man under suspicion of wanting to poison him. Gaston Phoebus also had an illegitimate son, Yvain, who was burned to death when his disguise as a "savage" (part of a wedding party prank) caught fire. The day, Tuesday, 28 January 1393, is known in history as Le Bal des Ardents. These were strange destinies, in which savagery and obscure forces operated side by side with courtly manners.

The literary world offered a number of pairs of writer fathers and sons. The phenomenon was new and interesting. We know much less about the lives of the poets of the time than we do about the princes, which means that we must turn to the poets themselves, rather than the archives, for information. A temptation to indulge in aubiography—a desire for self—appeared in French literature of the fourteenth century; it was in fact one of its principal characteristics. Family ties in the field of letters were also a sign that writing was no longer solely in the hands of monks and friars. It showed that for some time writing had been akin to a trade, passed on from father to son just as painting was in families of artists in the workshop tradition. In physical filiation among writers we see an aspect of fourteenth-century writing: it was a craft. In *Le Dit dou levrier,* Jean de Condé tells his readers:

Fius fui Bauduin de Condé,
S'est bien raisons k'en moi apere

> Aucune teche de mon pere
> Et un petitet de son sens.   (*Dits et contes*, 2:304, ll. 40–43)

> [I am the son of Baudoin de Condé. It is only just that certain of my father's qualities and a bit of his spirit should appear in me.]

A son ought to resemble his father. For the son, the mention of a minstrel father was a subtle way of establishing his own credentials through the use of a topos and an obligatory expression of modesty.

Thomas de Pizan and his daughter Christine offer a further example. Christine de Pizan deliberately invokes paternal filiation, but she rejects maternal filiation for an allegorical one. She insists on this point in *Le Livre de la mutacion de fortune*. She declares herself *le fils* (the son) of Thomas—all known manuscripts agree in this reading—and *la fille* (the daughter) of Nature:

> Filz de noble homme et renommé
> Fus, qui philosophe ert nommé.   (Vol. 1, ll. 171–72)

> [I am the son of a noble and well-known man, who was called a philosopher.]

But the power of her allegorical mother, Nature, "royne couronnee" [crowned queen] was such that she was born a woman. This complicated coming into possession of her father's inheritance of knowledge:

> et succeder
> Ne poz a l'avoir qui est pris
> En la fonteine de grant pris,
> Plus par coustume que par droit.   (Ll. 416–19)

> [and I could not inherit the wealth that is lodged in the precious fountain, more by custom than by right.]

Christine de Pizan saw custom as embodied in her birth mother, whom she contrasted with her father, who represented the law. In *Le Livre de la cité des dames*, Christine has Droiture (Rectitude) state:

> Ton pere, qui fu grant naturien et phillosophe, n'oppinoit pas que femmes vaulsissent pis par science apprendre, ains de ce qu'encline

te veoit aux lettres, si que tu sces, grant plaisir y prenoit. Mais l'op-
pinion femenine de ta mere, qui te vouloit occuper en fillasses
selonc l'usaige commun des femmes, fu cause de l'empeschement
que ne fus en ton enffance plus avant boutee es sciences et plus en
parfont.   (Pt. 2, chap. 36, p. 875)

[Your father, who was a great scientist and a philosopher, did not
believe that women were worth less by knowing science; rather, as
you know, he took great pleasure from seeing your inclination to
learning. The feminine opinion of your mother, however, who
wished to keep you busy with spinning and silly girlishness, following the common custom of women, was the major obstacle to
your being more involved in the sciences (Richards translation,
154–55).]

If filiation could make offspring learned (as with Christine de
Pizan), paternity might also smooth the way for a writer child. This
process was deliberate policy with Eustache Deschamps, in whose
works we see petitions passing from son to father (*Oeuvres complètes*,
8:96–97, no. 1433; and 8:187–88, no. 1480), then from the father to
the pope:

Tressaint pere, n'oubliez mie
Gillet mon filz, qu'il n'ait sa place
D'obtenir quelque chanonnie:
Veuillez lui faire vostre grace.
                        (5:317, no. 1038, ll. 31–34, envoi)

[Most Holy Father, do not forget Gillet, my son, so that he
may obtain some canonry. Deign to grant him your grace.]

We can see the same concern operating on a deeper level with the
Chevalier de La Tour Landry, who tells us he began to write in "l'an
mil trois cens soixante et onze" (1371). In his youth, he tells us, Love
made him a poet, "car en cellui temps je faisoye chançons, laiz et rondeaux, balades et virelayz, et chans nouveaux, le mieulx que je savoye"
(*Le Livre du Chevalier de La Tour Landry*, 2) [for in that time, I made
songs, lays, rondeaux, ballades and virelays, and new songs, as best I
could].

But the lady died, and the knight became sad and pensive. Individual human destiny mimicked the evolution of courtly lyric poetry from the love song of the twelfth and thirteenth centuries, placed under the sign of Hope, to the mournful lament and the didacticism that followed the death of the lady. That was the stance of the poets who followed Dante. In the case of the Chevalier de La Tour Landry, the poet no longer wrote for the lady but for his own daughters. One no longer sang; one taught: "Je me pensay que je feroye un livret, où je escrire feroye les bonnes meurs des bonnes dames et leurs biens faiz, à la fin de y prendre bon exemple et belle contenance et bonne manière. . . . Je leur feroye un livret pour aprendre à roumancer, affin que elles peussent aprendre et estudier, et veoir et le bien et le mal qui passé est, pour elles garder de cellui temps qui à venir est" (3–4) [I thought to myself that I would make a little book in which I would write the good ways of gentlewomen and their fine actions, so that one could take from them a good example, a handsome countenance, and good manners. . . . I would make «my daughters» a little book so that they can learn to read in French in order to learn, study, and see the good and the bad in past times and protect themselves in the times to come].

The people of this age were fond of reflecting on examples of fathers and sons. Such wisdom was at times banal, but it is interesting to see how it worked. Using the example of the biblical Rebecca and her two sons, Jacob and Esau, the Chevalier de La Tour Landry states: "Et ainsi ne sont pas les enffans d'un père et d'une mère d'une manière; car les uns aiment un mestier et une manière de oeuvre et les autres une autre" (164) [Hence the children of one father and one mother are not all alike, for some like one task and one occupation and the others like another.]

He also recalled the importance of a pure lineage: "car les enfants qui sont mal engendrez et qui ne sont de loyal mariage, ce sont ceulx par qui sont les guerres et par qui les ancesseurs sont perduz" (118–19) [for ill-conceived children and those not from a loyal marriage are the ones by whom wars arrive and by whom ancestors are forgotten].

This thought was both moral and political. Bastardy explained tyranny, which occurred when force took precedence over natural legitimacy. This was why France in the fourteenth and fifteenth centuries took a dim view of Italy, in particular of the Visconti rule in Milan. Philippe de Commynes remarks in his *Mémoires,* "Mais ilz ne font point grant differance en Italie d'ung enfant bastard à ung legitime" (3:15) [But they make no great difference in Italy between a bastard child and a legitimate one]. The question of fathers, of the spirit or of the flesh, involved questions of authority and inheritance. To keep to the literary domain, what, then, were the antecedents of the writers of the time, and what was their culture?

The Birth of an Art: Writer or Copyist, Clerk or Minstrel?

There was often a transfer of authority from birth fathers to symbolic fathers. For the writers of the fourteenth century, such symbolic fathers might be the persons for whom they wrote—patrons, the lady, friends—or the ones after whom they wrote—the *auctoritates,* their predecessors, their models. How did writers situate themselves in relation to those who came before, and how did they refer to themselves?

One word, *creator,* was prohibited for religious reasons: only God creates. Another word, *écrivain* (writer), was ambiguous. Yes, the word designated a person who writes, but especially in the physical sense; and so it was applied to copyists. The modern sense of *writer* as "author" begins to appear with Jean de Meun in *Le Roman de la Rose* in the thirteenth century. The contexts in which the term appears are interesting. Plato, Aristotle, and the great Greek and Arab mathematicians were "writers," but their *angin* (mind, intelligence) was *vain*—powerless—when it came to describing nature. Jean de Meun's rhyme *escrivain/vain* (vol. 2, ll. 16143–44) is significant. But monkeys could do as much had they been granted the gifts of speech and reason:

> et porroient estre escrivain.
> Il ne seroient ja si vain
> que tretuit ne s'asoutillassent.   (Ll. 17805–7)

> [they could be writers. They would never be so empty-headed that they might not exercise their wits (Dahlberg translation, 297).]

Escrivain also appears in the message of Genius, when that character in the *Roman de la Rose* draws a parallel between the physical activity of writing and the act of generation (l. 19605).

In the fourteenth century, writing really took place somewhere between the two extremes of the total sovereignty of the artist, an idea that was rejected, and concrete craftsmanship, the manual labor of the scribe, which was becoming a thing of the past. These two orientations defined values that continued to be contrasted in literature: labor and inspiration, the humility of the artisan and the artist's pride. The minstrel stood at one end of the spectrum; at the other, there was the French *poète* who had appropriated a title once reserved for the ancients.

The *ménestrel* (minstrel) was a later version of the jongleur. As the etymology of the word indicates, the minstrel had come to have a "ministry": he was attached to a lord, a noble house, a prince, or—an innovation at the time—a wealthy merchant. This was the situation of Jean de Condé, who was attached to the person of the "good Count" Guillaume de Hainaut, whose death he mourned and whose generosity he sorely missed:

> Jeans de Condet, qui estoit
> De son maisnage et qui viestoit
> Des robes de ses escuyers;
> Le gentieus quens de Hainnuiers
> Lui a dou sien douné maint don.
>
> (*Li Dis dou Boin Conte Willaume,* in
> *Dits et contes,* 2:295, ll. 165–69)

> [Jean de Condé, who was part of his «Guillaume's» household and wore the raiment of his squires; the noble count of the Hennuyers made him many gifts from his own wealth.]

Jean de Condé calls his inimitable patron "the father of the minstrels." Jean de Le Mote had a similar status. He wrote a funeral lament for the same Guillaume de Hainaut (*Li Regret Guillaume, comte de Hainaut,* 1339) on the command of Gauillaume's daughter, Philippa de Hainaut, later the protectress of the young Jean Froissart, and the following year he found a new protector in Simon de Lille, a Parisian *grand bourgeois* and goldsmith to the king. In that same year (1340), Jean de Le Mote wrote two works for Simon, *Le Parfait du paon* and *La Voie d'enfer et de paradis.* The first of these works "perfected"—that is, completed—a tale based on the legend of Alexander the Great begun by Jacques de Longuyon in *Les Voeux du paon* and continued by Jean Le Court, called Brisebare, in his *Restor du paon.* In Jean de Le Mote's work Alexander takes part in a ballade-writing contest during a truce and wins second prize, the first prize going to a true romance heroine, Clarete, the daughter of the king of Melide. This was how the epic was interpreted in the fourteenth century in the *puys* —literary associations—of northern France: the depiction of literary life took precedence over that of war. In this text, Jean de Le Mote names his patron on several occasions, presenting him in these terms:

> Li boins Symons de Lille—ou Dix face garant!—
> N'est pas de ciex moquieurs comme j'ai dit devant.
> Anchois ainme le fait—bien est apparissant—
> Quant il me livre vivre, chambre et clerc escrisant
> Pour faire li biax dis; d'el ne le vois servant.
>
> (*Le Parfait du paon,* laisse 50, ll. 1453–57)

[The good Simon de Lille—may God protect him!—is not of those mockers of whom I have spoken. To the contrary, he loves poetry, as is well demonstrated by the fact that he gives me room and board and a clerk who writes, so that I can make fine compositions; that is all my service to him.]

Jean de Le Mote took obvious pride in the increased specialization of his function. He states that he does not copy; he composes, he "makes." He is *un faiseur*: in his *Méditations* (*Poésies*, 1:89, l. 9), Gilles Li Muisis calls him one of the best "makers"—"et des milleurs faiseurs tenus." Jean de Le Mote admits to two fathers: God, the heavenly Father, and the terrestrial father who recognizes him as his son, Simon de Lille. *La Voie d'enfer et de paradis* begins:

> Che libre fay premierement
> Ou nom du Roi du firmament,
>   . . . .

Et puis, en la mondaine vie
Le fais, car desirs m'en maistrie,
Pour l'onneur et la courtoisie
D'un bourgeois, douls et reverent
Qui mes maistres est, quoi c'on die,
Symon de Lille.   (Stanza 3, ll. 25–26, 30–35)

[I make this book first in the name of the King of heaven.
. . . And then I make it for what pertains to life on earth,
for I desire to do so for the honor and the courtesy of a
bourgeois, gentle and venerable, who is my master, whatever one might say: Simon de Lille.]

Where his living was concerned, Jean de Le Mote was a minstrel:
he lived in the house of Simon de Lille, who fed him. By his specific
function and his nascent pride, he had special status. Eustache Deschamps seems to have been the first to apply the honorific term *poète*
to an author who wrote in French, in this case, his symbolic father,
Guillaume de Machaut. We may note his need for a gloss, the term
faiseur, a synonymic doublet that highlights the special sense of the
word *poète*:

Noble poete et faiseur renommé
Plus qu'Ovide vray remede d'amours,
Qui m'a nourry et fait maintes douçours.
                    (*Oeuvres complètes*, 3:259, no. 447, ll. 3–5)

[Noble poet and renowned writer, more than Ovid a true
remedy for love «an allusion to Ovid's *Remedia amoris,* the
antidote to his *Arts of Love*» who raised me and showed me
many favors.]

An anonymous work giving rules for versification, *Les Règles de la
seconde rhétorique,* presents Eustache Morel (that is, Eustache Deschamps) as the "nepveux de maistre Guillaume de Machault" (14). As
is known, the word *neveux* (nephew) had a range of meanings in
Latin and Old French. Here *Les Règles* speaks less of blood kinship
than of symbolic filiation. Machaut was the poetry master for the en-

tire generation writing during the last quarter of the fourteenth century. He consciously took on that role. He proposed models: *Le Remede de fortune* offered a characteristic sampling of lyric forms in seven pieces set to music (seven, like the seven days of the week or the seven planets, the image of harmony) ranging from the most complicated form, the lai, to the seemingly simplest, the rondeau.

His sampling opens and closes with cyclical forms, since in the lai the first and last stanzas are constructed on an identical rhyme scheme with the same meter, and in the rondeau the initial refrain returns at the end, closing the circle. This was another image of harmony, offered in a carefully calculated presentation that hid its didacticism behind love songs. The *Voir-Dit* is proof of the thought that Guillaume de Machaut put into his works. In the prologue, which precedes a list of all his works, he even offers a body of precepts, the first French "Art of Poetry." He organized his work with care, as seen in the famous dictum at the head of one manuscript (Fonds français 1584, Bibliothèque nationale, Paris): "Vesci l'ordenance que Guillaume de Machaut wet qu'il ait en son livre" [This is the order that Guillaume de Machaut wants there to be in his book].

Eustache Deschamps gave two indications that he recognized in Guillaume de Machaut the figure of a master teacher, an exemplary father, and an authority. The first is the dignified title of *poète* that he accords him; the second is the refrain, "La mort Machaut, le noble rethorique" in the double ballade deploring Machaut's death (*Oeuvres complètes*, 1:243–44, no. 123; and 1:245–46, no. 124). Until the fourteenth century, funereal laments in poetry usually had as their subject a nobleman, a heroic warrior, or a great lord. There may be an exception in Provençal in the *planh* (*plainte*; lament) that Giraut de Bornelh wrote for Raimbaut d'Orange (no. 76). But Raimbaut was both a prince and a poet. It seems, then, that Eustache Deschamps was, once again, an innovator: for the first time in French, a poet wrote a lament for a poet. Moreover, we would have to wait until 1466, when Simon Gréban wrote his *Complaincte de la mort de maistre Jacques Millet qui composa la Destruction de Troye,* before the eulogy of one artist for another flourished as a genre. This combination of traits is significant.

What were the socially defined spaces in the terrain that opened up between the minstrel and the "poet" (who attained that status only when recognized as such by his "sons," that is, by posterity)? There were many terms for an author: *dicteur* (someone who composed, not someone who dictated), *acteur, facteur, faitistre, collecteur, versifieur, reciteur* (roughly, author, maker, poet, compiler, versifier, reciter). Writers' functions and posts varied as well: secretary to a prince, royal officeholder, man of the church. Later ages found it convenient to speak of this authorial figure as a *clerc-écrivain* (clerk-writer). The differences between this clerk and the minstrel lay essentially in two domains: before the fact, in the writer's relationship to the book, and after the fact, in the way the book was produced and read and in the author's dependence on patrons.

Unlike the minstrel, the clerk-writer did not rely on one protector for his sustenance. He had a function, a post: he was a bailiff, like Eustache Deschamps, or a canon, like Guillaume de Machaut and Jean Froissart. He had more than one protector, not only in succession, when one died and was replaced by another, but at the same time. Writing to his lady in the *Voir-Dit,* Guillaume de Machaut speaks of his *livre,* the collection of all his writings: "Mais il est en plus de XX. pieces; car je l'ay fait faire pour aucun de mes seigneurs" (*Le Livre du Voir-Dit,* letter 10 of the lover, p. 69) [But it is in more than twenty pieces, for I had it made for one of my lords].

The conflict of allegiance typical of the lovesick clerk, which Machaut had eliminated by making his lady his lord, returns stronger than ever in the second part of this text, where it signals the impossibility of that love in the eyes of the great. Christine de Pizan also had multiple protectors, and she used their number as a strategy to guarantee her a degree of political freedom and to enhance her economic advantage. An author's work gained value if he or she was solicited from all sides, and Christine stressed the many offers she received from England and from Italy.

More and more, clerk-writers managed their production as one would a commercial venture. Commercial images crop up in many works; in Jean Froissart they overflow. One must be *pourveü* (furnished) with poems in order to respond immediately to a request. In *La Prison amoureuse* the poet, designated emblematically under the name of Flos, writes to his patron, Wenceslas of Brabant ("Rose" in the text): "Rose, tres chiers compains et grans amis, vous m'avés escript que aucun dittié nouvellement fet et ordonné je vous vosisse envoiier. Sachiés que au jour que vostres lettres me vinrent, je n'en estoie point pourveüs" (letter 6 of Flos, p. 103) [Rose, most dear companion and great friend, you have written to me to ask that I please send you a piece newly done and composed. Know that the day your letter reached me I had none in my possession]. Or, again: "Je vous envoie trois balades faites assés nouvellement, en l'absence d'un lay, car je n'en sui pas pourveüs tant qu'en present" (letter 9 of Flos, p. 155) [I send you three ballades done quite recently, in the absence of a lay, for I am not furnished with them «I do not have any in reserve» at the moment].

Writing, which had the advantage of ease of conservation over oral presentation, enabled poets to resolve one of the contradictions born of a conflict between their aesthetic and their social condition. They wanted to write out of *sentement* (in harmony with an experience; with genuine feeling), but they also wanted to produce on command. Only writing and the interplay with deferred experience that it authorized permitted them to honor that dual necessity. Thus, when they found themselves faced with the contradiction of having to sing when they felt like weeping, these poets turned to the image of the minstrel. On two occasions in the *Voir-Dit*, Guillaume de Machaut adapted a proverb: "Tel fois chante li menestriers que c'est de touz li plus courreciés" (*Proverbes français antérieurs au XVe siècle*, no. 2315) [At times the minstrel sings when he is the unhappiest of men].

First, in order to indicate the tension that governs his writing—a tension in danger of being extinguished when his lady's love no longer fuels it—Guillaume de Machaut writes that he "ressemble le menestrel qui chante en place et n'y a plus courrecié de lui" (*Le Livre du Voir-Dit,* letter 21 of the lover, p. 241) [resembles the minstrel who sings and is the most unhappy of all]. He returns to the image in letter 25: "Mais je ressemble le menestrel qui chante telle foi en la place, et il n'y a plus dolent de lui" (p. 263) [But I am like the minstrel who sings of his fidelity in the square, and there is no one more unhappy than he].

We know how Jean Froissart resolved the problem: he stocked up on pieces he had composed in the heat of the moment for later revision. He writes in *La Prison amoureuse*:

> Jusques a trois balades fis,
> Selonc le matere et l'avis
> Que j'avoie lors pour le tamps
> Et dou quel je sui bien sentans.　　　　　(Ll. 2030–33)

[I made three ballades in harmony with the matter and the impressions that I felt at that time.]

When he had written these ballades, Froissart put them away in a coffer for safekeeping:

> A fin que, quant je les voloie
> Envoiier, donner ou proumettre,
> Tost peüisse sus le main mettre.　　　　　(Ll. 2119–21)

[So that, when I wanted to send them, give them, or promise them, I could put my hands on them quickly.]

It was the same with a lay:

> Encore entrepris a faire
> Un lay, quoi que fust dou parfaire,
> Selonc le matere et le tamps
> Le quel j'estoie adont sentans.　　　　　(Ll. 2122–25)

[I also began a lay—whatever its completion might be—in harmony with the matter and the moment, just as I felt them then.]

Christine de Pizan resolved the same tension by what she called an *amende volontaire,* or free acquiescence to constraint. The envoi concluding the ballade that serves as a prologue to her collection *Cent Ballades d'amant et de dame* states:

> Prince, bien voy qu'il se vauldroit mieux taire
> Que ne parler a gré; voy cy comment
> Payer m'en fault d'amende volontaire,
> Cent balades d'amoureux sentement.   (32)

> [Prince, I see clearly that it would be better to remain silent than to speak only as one wishes; that is why I must compose, in payment as a volontary forfeit, one hundred ballades of loving sentiment.]

For these poets, the sensation of laughing through one's tears that all writers have experienced was the special province of the jongleur. It was the sign of a dependency that they dreamed of escaping. Alain Chartier states: "Tempus enim ridendi et tempus flendi. Qui secus facit non viri, sed joculatoris vacat officio" (*Dialogus familiaris,* 250) [There is a time for laughing and a time for weeping. Whoever does not act that way behaves not as a man but as a jongleur]. In the contemporary French translation of the *Dialogus* this passage runs: "Car il est aucunnesfoiz temps de rire et autresfoiz de plorer, et qui autrement le fait, il doit plus tost estre appelé jangleur que joueur" (251) [For there is at some times occasion to laugh and at other times to weep, and anyone who does otherwise should rather be called a trickster than a musician].

The change is significant, since it refers not to playing and singing but to trickery—*jangleur* in Old French meant liar, compulsive talker, person given to mockery. Not until François Villon, a sublime *jongleur,* were laughter and tears taken as the expression of a split personality rather than uniquely the sign of a social condition or a desire to deceive.

One of the conquests of the book was avoidance of constraint by the use of deferral. This procedure profoundly transformed the relationship of the clerk-writer to his activity. Remuneration remained a pressing problem, but it did not necessarily confine the poet to a role as entertainer. Eustache Deschamps could remind the king of the two hundred francs he had been promised four years earlier:

Et le faictes ordonner le premier
Affin qu'il puist avoir ses deux cens frans,
Ou il convient qu'il deviengne bergier
Et qu'il garde brebis aval les champs;
Plus ne fera chançons, livre ne chans,
Ainsois joura de la turelurette.

(*Oeuvres complètes*, 4:294–95, no. 788, ll. 17–22)

[And give first priority to the order for him to have his two hundred francs, or he will have to turn shepherd and keep sheep in the fields; he will no longer make airs, books, or songs but will play the pipes.]

Reading for the Last Draft of Wine

Poets did not play musical instruments (a frequent sense of the word *menestrel*), and they were not entertainers. They saw themselves as advisors of princes and as sages. Guillaume de Machaut takes that position in *Le Confort d'Ami*, as does Eustache Deschamps in *Le Lay de plour* (*Oeuvres complètes*, 2:306–14, no. 310), in *Le Lay du roy* (2:314–23, no. 311) and in a number of his ballades. Christine de Pizan assumed the same pose. What the clerk-writer produced was books, not performances. Here again Jean Froissart gives us the prototype, as demonstrated by an anecdote related in *Le Dit dou florin*. The poet arrived at the court of Gaston Phoebus in Orthez already provided with a book of his composition—*Meliador*. The romance of the "chevalier au soleil d'or" [knight of the golden sun; l. 296) had been written on the command of Wenceslas of Brabant, but Wenceslas had died without seeing the completed work:

Et le livre me fist ja faire
Par tres grant amoureus afaire,
Comment qu'il ne le veïst onques.

(*Le Dit dou florin*, in *"Dits" et "Débats,"* ll. 307–9)

[And he had me do the book «and showed» great interest, although he never saw it.]

This means that Wenceslas had had no opportunity to reward the poet. For nearly three months, Froissart read seven pages of his *Meliador* to Gaston Phoebus every evening at midnight:

> Quant leü avoie un septier
> De foeilles et a sa plaisance,
> Li contes avoit ordenance
> Que le demorant de son vin,
> Qui venoit d'un vaissiel d'or fin,
> En moi sonnant, c'est chose voire,
> Le demorant me faisoit boire. (Ll. 368–74)

[When I had read some seven pages for his pleasure, the count commanded, to the sound of an instrument—this is the truth—that I drink the remainder of his wine, which came in a vessel of pure gold.]

When Froissart had finished reading the entire work, Gaston Phoebus paid him. That is, he rewarded his entertainment, but he did not buy the book. Froissart was disappointed, as he showed in an incidental remark:

> Et mon livre qu'il m'ot laissié,
> (Ne sçai se ce fu de coeur lié),
> Mis en Avignon sans damage. (Ll. 387–89)

[And my book, which he had left me—I know not if it was with a joyful heart—I took off safe and sound to Avignon.]

The gracious concession of the wine left in the count's goblet and the remuneration of the poet's performance demoted him to the rank of a minstrel. Gaston Phoebus had not acknowledged Froissart's book as an object worthy of possession. The count was not acting as a "modern" prince in this exchange, and in fact, archival documents show him to have been a miserly ruler.

But there were other princes who bought books and collected them as beautiful objects and—even better for the poets—as texts. Jean de Berry, Louis d'Anjou, and Louis d'Orléans all appreciated beautiful books; Charles V loved good texts, especially ones useful for government. Many of the Valois had a taste for books, as did members of all the princely houses of the age. In *Le Jugement dou roy de Behaingne,* Guillaume de Machaut shows Jean de Luxembourg in his château at Durbuy (now in the Belgian province of Luxembourg), having "the battle of Troy" read to him:

> En moult grant joie
> Estoit assis sur un tapis de soie,
> Et ot un clerc que nommer ne saroie
> Qui li lisoit la bataille de Troie.
> (Oeuvres, vol. 1, ll. 1472–75)

[In very great contentment he was seated on a silk rug, and some clerk whom I cannot name was reading to him the battle of Troy (Palmer translation, 65).]

Guillaume de Machaut tells us more about Jean de Luxembourg:

> Et d'Amours
> Congnoist il tous les assaus, les estours,
> Les bien, les maus, les plaintes et les plours
> Mieux qu'Ovides qui en sot tous les tours.   (Ll. 1324–27)

[Of Love, he knows all the assaults, the skirmishes, the joys, the pains, the sorrowing and moaning, better than Ovid himself, who knew all its doings (Palmer translation, 59).]

The Court of Love

Court life had a literary savor. Other princes went even further, adopting the figure of a poet themselves. This was an attitude not unknown in earlier literature: we need only think of Guillaume IX (William of Aquitaine) and Thibaut de Champagne. During the fourteenth and fifteenth centuries, the fashion developed, reaching such high-ranking lords as the knight-poets Jehan de Garencières and Oton de Grandson, the circle around Louis d'Orléans that produced *Le Livre des Cent Balades* and its responses, and Wenceslas of Brabant.

The following century was dominated by the looming figure of Charles d'Orléans and the engaging figure of René d'Anjou. For an entire society, poetry had become a serious game.

When Charles VI founded the Court of Love there was an institution to bear witness to this game. The Cour d'Amour was created on 6 January 1400, the feast of the Epiphany; its charter was "published" (which meant, as the text stated, read in public) on St. Valentine's Day of the same year in the Hôtel d'Artois, the Paris residence of the duke of Burgundy. Charles VI founded the court at the initiative of Philippe (le Hardi), duc de Bourgogne, and Louis, duc de Bourbonnais. It was created under the aegis of the two virtues of *humilité* and *loyauté* (humility and fidelity) "à l'honneur, louange, recommandacion et service de toutes dames et damoiselles" [to the honor, praise, commendation, and service of all ladies and maids). It was ruled over by its "prince," Pierre de Hauteville (b. 1376, d. at Lille 10 October 1448), the author of the court's charter and a protégé of the duke of Burgundy. As a literary and festive association to honor love, the purpose of the Cour d'Amour was to "tenir joieuse feste de puy d'amours" [hold joyful festivities as an association of love] on the first Sunday of each month and on certain other dates selected for their symbolic value—St. Valentine's Day, a day during the month of May, and one of the five feasts of the Virgin.

When a manuscript of this charter was discovered in the eighteenth century, scholars then and in the following century sought models for such an institution. Was it related to the courts of love of the troubadours? No, because in reality those courts were an invention of Jean de Nostredame, the brother of Michel, the famous astrologer, in the sixteenth century. Was it an allegorical dramatization of the court of the god of Love, as Friedrich Diez believed, and, after him, Gaston Paris? Or was it a tribunal, a law court of love, like other "courts" of the time and like the later example described in the *Arrêts d'Amour* of Martial d'Auvergne?

In point of fact, the direct model for the organization of the Cour d'Amour was the literary associations known as *puys* to which the court's charter explicitly refers, and perhaps as well the *chambres de rhétorique,* "courts" that decided literary stylistic questions. Pierre de Hauteville came from northern France, where such societies flourished, and the activities on the agenda of the Cour d'Amour—the composition of ballades on a given refrain, writing *serventois* (moral poems in stanzas) in honor of the Virgin, dinners, parties, masses, debates on amorous subjects "pour plaisant passetempz"—were precisely those of the *puys.* The Cour d'Amour had another dimension, however, that likened it to the many chivalric orders that were created and flourished during the fourteenth and fifteenth centuries: its statutes were followed by a listing of the names and heraldic devices of its members. The Cour d'Amour—and this is one reason why it was such a complex institution—was a cross between an urban, bourgeois model (the *puys*) and a chivalric model (the orders of knighthood). It was intended not only to produce poetry and provide occasions for games but also to pass laws—in play, of course—and to guarantee social conduct in realms that were, in fact, not so much amorous as they were moral. What is fascinating about the creation of this institution is thus its ambivalence. The game was played using a serious, even solemn, juridical language; painstaking codification was an amusement but also a sign of anxiety.

This ambivalence resided, first, in the very circumstances of the creation of the court. It was founded, the charter tells us, "pour passer partie du tempz plus gracieusement" [to pass some of the time more gracefully] during an epidemic of plague. Like the company of well-born young people in Boccaccio's *Decameron,* which takes place with the plague of 1348 as its background, the aim of the assembled company was to find a pleasurable pastime. The analogy reflects another aspect of the Court of Love, which is its literary nature. In painful circumstances (the broader background was the Hundred Years' War; the immediate environment, mentioned explicitly in the charter, was a wave of the plague), life was made to resemble literature. A voluntarist and abstract definition of self was affirmed, codified, and fixed in place, whatever reality might ultimately be. That affirmation was all the stronger because the gap had widened between a self-image dreamed of or deliberately displayed and the real practice of court milieus, bourgeois circles, and royal functionaries at the turn of the fourteenth to the fifteenth century.

The Court of Love was a means for pursuing a variety of aims. First, it was a way of restating a definition of nobility—not the original definition but the one found in Jean de Meun's *Le Roman de la Rose.* The only nobility that counted was that of the heart and of one's lifestyle. (Here we can sense the influence of members of the bourgeoisie and the royal functionaries.) The new institution worked to redefine social status within its own province, the service of love. In this fashion, the names of the members, the charter states, were to be written in the register of love in order of their function in that court, "sans avoir tant soit peu de regard a plus ancienne noblesse, auctorité, vaillance renommee, puissance presente ou richesse" [without even the least regard to the oldest noblility, authority, reputation for bravery, present power, or wealth]. Such was the virtue of humility, under whose power the Court of Love was placed. What we see happening here is the creation of *notables,* in the root sense of those worthy of being noted in the registers of love and whose names, thus noted, must be passed on to posterity. Renown became a possible substitute for nobility of birth; *renom* might surpass *nom.*

It is easy to measure the degree of deviation between this desire and the heavy weight of social stratification and, perhaps even more, the weight of clans in a divided kingdom. The prince of Love gave first place to the *grands conservateurs* of the Cour d'Amour, who were listed in an order that respected their social status. After them came the hierarchy of the court itself, which had its prince, ministers, presidents, prelates, lords, and counselors of various sorts. Moreover, the Burgundian orientation of the Cour d'Amour was obvious, influencing its ideal moral definition. Burgundian influence became even more pronounced as time went by. Thus Christine de Pizan was soon led to create a new order devoted to love—the Ordre de la Rose—under the aegis of the duc d'Orléans (1401). In her *Dit de la Rose,* Christine describes the founding of this order. The central figure in the poem, the goddess Loyalty, reminds her listeners of the nature of nobility:

Je n'entens pas par bas lignaige
Le vilain, mais par vil courage.
(Oeuvres poétiques, vol. 2, ll. 338–39)

[By common I don't mean low birth, but rather lowly heart
and mind (Willard translation, 163).]

The two groups affirmed the same order of ideas; what differed was
the political faction they supported.

The other virtue that entered into the emblem of both the Court
of Love and Christine de Pizan's Order of the Rose was *loyauté* (loyalty, fidelity). In a shift characteristic of the institution, however, this
fidelity was no longer concentrated in the domain of arms and warfare but was focused on the service of love. Even there the problem
was current, and the real situation was troubled. The founding of the
Cour d'Amour occurred in the middle of the quarrel concerning *Le
Roman de la Rose,* a quarrel (which continued into the sixteenth century under the name of the *querelle des femmes*) debated on both a
moral and a literary plane. Christine de Pizan launched the debate
with her *Epistre au Dieu d'Amours,* where she reproached Jean de
Meun for having spoken ill of women. Some members of the Cour
d'Amour—Gontier Col, "notaire et secretaire du roy," his brother
Pierre Col, "chanoine de Paris et de Tournay," and Jean de Montreuil,
"prevost de Saint Pierre de Lille"—sided with Jean de Meun, attack-
ing women and opposing Christine in the ensuing debate. Some
members of that same institution founded to honor women were
even known to have attempted female abductions and kidnappings.
The paradox was striking.

Moreover, the question of *loyauté en amour*—fidelity in love—ran
through the entire century. The theme was stated explicitly in *Les
Cent Ballades* of Jean le Sénéchal and his friends (1389). This collection presented a game of choosing sides on the topic, "Vaut-il mieux
en amour être loyal ou non?" [Is it better to be faithful in love or
not?]. Typical of the attitudes displayed in the responses to this question was the declaration of Jean de Berry, later a member of the Cour
d'Amour, in the refrain of his ballade: "On peut l'un dire et l'autre

doit on faire" [One can say one thing, and one should do the other].
One's word was no longer a pledge; signs could be twisted. What
makes an institution like the Court of Love endlessly interesting is
this sort of interplay between what was said and what was left unsaid.
We can also see the malaise of a society seeking to conceal the fact
that it was evolving by proclaiming a morality contradicted by its attitudes.

The Cour d'Amour was in reality based on a game of role-playing
whose principal aim was the acquisition of praise and renown. The
game was played under the gaze of the ancestors—the fathers—who
lent authority to the rules and mechanisms of the game. A theory of
love underlies this institution, derived from the courtly morality
stated and glorified in the lyric poetry of the troubadours and the
twelfth-century romance and codified by André le Chapelain in his
Traité de l'amour courtois. It stated that love is the source of all virtues.
The love of a lady and of only one lady—"pour l'amour d'une" [for
love of one] was the acknowledged formula—brought honor to all
women. Thus no one could be of worth, could be prized, who did
not love. Love permitted men to surpass themselves; it urged them
on to grand actions in all domains. By that logic, to say that one
loved was to assert one's merit.

It is clear that the Court of Love aimed at maintaining values that
were declining in the real world. Chief among these was of course
loyauté (fidelity), undermined by a dual language reflected both in
texts and in action. Another declining value was joy: the court sought
to enable its members to "trouver esveil de nouvelle joye" [find the
awakening of new joy]. The act of foundation was thus conceived as
a therapy that would permit an entire society in crisis to escape a sentiment—melancholy—that was becoming predominant in both life
and aesthetics. A third value that the court defended was stability.
The charter aimed at constructing an edifice beyond the reach of
Fortune and her wheel. A search for stable governance was undoubt-
edly the reason for the almost maniacal profusion of minute details
and numbers in the charter. This care was ironic, however: the char-

ter's painstaking, bourgeois accounting methods stood in stark contrast to its exaltation of the older values of honor, generosity, and joyful and spendthrift outlay. The court clerks registered the weight of the silver crowns to be offered to the winners of the poetry contests, gave the names of the copyists who wrote down the ballades and noted their pay, and specified who paid for the paper.

This was all done in the interests of keeping a record of what was done within the institution. What mattered was that the name of the Court of Love be known; it was erecting a statue for the benefit of later generations. The game of love was played to the gallery rather than in the lady's chamber (the ladies were mute; their "judgments" were not recorded). The game of love had become representation. Loving was less important than declaring that one loved; one must sing of love's torments, not die of them. Christine de Pizan was fully aware of the increased literary dimension of lovers' laments. In her *Le Debat de deux amans* (*Oeuvres poétiques*, vol. 2, ll. 942–44), one lady states that such an attitude was merely "usage" [custom] and that people spoke thus of love out of "rigolage" [amusement], for fun and to pass the time. This was a society in search of entertainment. Christine de Pizan continues, suggesting, but with prudence, that perhaps "jadis . . . en l'ancien temps" [once . . . in the old days], there had been true lovers who died of love for their ladies. "Today" that is no longer the case, Christine states, nor was it true "yesterday"—by which she means a hundred years earlier. Lovers imitate the behavior of lovers in fiction; their pains are written in the romances (Christine cites *Le Roman de la Rose*) "et proprement desciptes / A longue prose" [and well described in lengthy prose (ll. 959–60)].

Thus contemporaries noted the literary dimension of the institution of the Court of Love, as seen in the models of behavior that it preached and sought to establish and in the works that it produced. To acquire worth one had to love, and to love, in that theory of love, meant to sing. But what is striking about the charter of the Cour d'Amour, and what anchors it deeply in the moral and literary problematics of the fourteenth and fifteenth centuries, is that "song" and poetic composition were exclusively conceived of as registered, written down. The new memory was paper. Thus the prince of Love was responsible for the "lieu de ce royaume [où] seront mis en garde le registre des armes, les papiers des balades et autres fais de rethorique, sy tost que plains seront d'escripture, pour les monstrer en temps a venir quant it plaira a ceulz qui le requerront et vaurront" [place in this kingdom where the registry of coats of arms and the papers of the ballades and other documents of rhetoric will be kept, as soon as they are covered with writing, in order to show them on future occasions when it shall please those who ask for them and want them].

The fact that ballades were noted down had consequences for their literary appreciation. They were scrutinized for the "vice de fausse rime" [the defect of faulty rhymes] and for "reditte trop longue ou trop courte ligne" [too long a repetition or lines too short], because, as the prince remarked, since the ballades that won prizes were "enregistrées en noz amoureux registres" [noted in our registers of love], their defects would be clearly visible. This meant that literary productions needed to be judged not only according to a moral *loyauté* (fairness), "sans avoir regard par faveur a hautesse de prince ou noblesse" [without regard or favor to rank of prince or noble] but also according to formal, legalistic rules specified in the treatises on rhetoric that insisted on proper rhymes and exact meters and rejected redundancy.

Jean de Renti, a mid-thirteenth-century trouvère from the Artois, criticized the Puy d'Arras, objecting that the judges had been influenced by kinship and social prestige and had awarded the victor's crown to asses. The Cour d'Amour hoped to protect itself from favoritism and ignorance, and it sought to leave a spotless record. For similar reasons, the questions to be debated had to be submitted in writing. The challenger and the defender each had to choose a color of ink (any color but black) and keep to it. Thus the questions that the presiding officers were to adjudicate, handing down their decisions on St. Valentine's Day, were submitted in a very carefully specified material form. What is more, any who broke one of the rules of the court to compose, or have others compose, defamatory writings against ladies past or present would have their coats of arms reproduced in ash gray in the registers. "Et nientmains, son nom et seurnom demorroient escripz sur icellui son escu, paint de couleur de cendres, affin que la gloire de sa renommee apparust aux regardans estre estainte et mauditte generamment par toutes terres" [And furthermore, his name and surname will remain written on his escutcheon, painted with the color of ashes, so that the glory of his fame shall appear to viewers to be extinguished and cursed everywhere in all lands]. Even disgrace must leave a trace.

The Cour d'Amour reflected a fashion and responded to a need. In only a few years, the institution of the Ordre de la Dame Blanche à l'écu vert (Order of the White Lady with the Green Escutcheon), founded for the defense of widows by Jean II le Meingre, called Boucicaut, was followed by that of the Cour d'Amour, which included members of the *confrérie* instituted by Boucicaut, and, within the year, by that of the Ordre de la Rose. All such groups were part of an immense cultural movement that included the *puys*, the *chambres de rhétorique*, and the new orders. The Cour d'Amour was by far the largest institution: its charter lists more than six hundred names in the manuscript in the Bibliothèque nationale in Paris (Fonds français 5233). The fashion was even reflected in parodies. Eustache Deschamps wrote a poem, "D'un beau dit de ceuls qui contreuvent nouvelles bourdes et mensonges" (*Oeuvres complètes*, 7:347–60, no. 1404) [A fine poem for those who think up new falsehoods and lies], that commanded—in jest—the formation of a parliament to plan May festivities, to be convened at Epernay on 16–17 October 1400. He also wrote a ballade with the refrain, "Pour compte de ses bourdes rendre" (7:361–62, no. 1405) [To tell about its falsehoods], that imagines convening a yearly parliament at Lens in Artois during the month of May. By 1400, the values defended by the Cour d'Amour had already been undermined, weakened by betrayal or derision.

Eustache Deschamps and Christine de Pizan attempted to take stock of the vacuum (or at least the ebbing tide) that the various codes of rules, the membership numbers, and the legalism of such groups tended to conceal. Later texts clarified the collapse of the body of doctrine on which the courts of love were based. Thus, while earlier "toute femme qui souhaite avoir les louanges du monde est tenue de s'adonner à l'amour" [any woman desirous of winning the world's praises is bound to devote herself to love (Willard translation, 261)], as judgment 12 of André le Chapelain's *Traité de l'amour courtois* reminds us (bk. 2, chap. 7), Alain Chartier's *La Belle Dame sans mercy,* written in 1424, shows the lady refusing not only to love but also to receive the homage of being loved. It is understandable that Chartier's book caused a scandal. Some of the many responses to *La Belle Dame sans mercy* were composed at Tournai, the city of the prince of Love, Pierre de Hauteville. The game of courtly love was no longer playable. This was also the conclusion, from another point of view, of Antoine de La Sale's *Jehan de Saintré.* The treason of the Dame des Belles Cousines and the infidelity that led her to reject the love of a young knight in favor of a fat abbot who mocked arms completed the destruction of the myth.

The Court of Love had attempted to make use of an institution that gave a predominant place to ritual in order to maintain a social cohesion and a doctrinal coherence threatened by centrifugal forces of all sorts—political, social, and ideological. To accept that challenge by equating life to literature—"to stylize love," as Johan Huizinga wrote (128)—was the mark of an epoch that sought to write of itself as a way to survive. Love of books became love of literature.

4 | *The Sadness When All Has Been Said*

Writers of the fourteenth century were acutely aware of living in a time of crisis in literary materials. That crisis had appeared in the thirteenth century, and it found its clearest expression—some years apart—in lyric poetry and the romance, the two great contemporary traditions in the French language.

Gui d'Ussel put the problem regarding lyric poetry this way at the beginning of the thirteenth century:

> Mas re no trob q'autra vez dit no sia.
>
> > (*Les Poésies,* first text by Gui, l. 6)
>
> [But I find nothing that others have not already said.]

Huon de Méry echoes Gui's complaint of a lack of narrative materials, referring in particular to Chrétien de Troyes, in *Li Tournoiemenz Antecrist*:

> Mes qui bien treuve pleins est d'ire,
> Quant il n'a de matire point.
> Joliveté semont et point
> Mon cuer de dire aucun bel dit;
> Mes n'ai de quoi; car tot est dit,
> Fors ce qui de novel avient.   (Ll. 4–9)

[But anyone who composes well is full of sadness when he has no material. Gaity commands my heart and urges it to say some fine thing; but I have nothing, for all is said except what is newly happening.]

The thirteenth century, however, saw a profound renewal of literary material, thanks to *Le Roman de la Rose*. That work clearly stated its optimistic awareness of founding a new genre. Guillaume de Lorris declares:

> Le matire est et bonne et neuve.   (Vol. 1, l. 39)
>
> [Its matter is good and new (Dahlberg translation, 31).]

Similarly, Jean Renart affirms in his own *Roman de la Rose* (the *Guillaume de Dole*) that the work "est une novele chose" [is a new thing], and Jean Bodel boasts of his *Chanson des Saisnes* that it contains "riches vers nouviaus" [rich new verse], an expression that he rhymed with his name, "Jehans Bodiaus."

The fourteenth century was the successor to the thirteenth in two ways: it inherited the narrative and lyric materials that the earlier century was aware of having exhausted, and it inherited the *Roman de la Rose*. The fundamental importance of that text, in the period that interests us here, is expertly analyzed by Pierre-Yves Badel in his study, *Le Roman de la Rose au XIVe siècle*. We might say that the fourteenth century replaced love of the Rose with a love of the *Roman de la Rose*. A century of literary reflexivity—of taking the very act of writing as the object of writing—the fourteenth was also a century of the love of books, especially of that particular book. It was an age of literature at one remove, at the second degree. As Pierre-Yves Badel puts it, there was a shift from an "état spontané" [spontaneous state] in French literature to an "état réflexif" (93) [reflective state].

This painful awareness of a crisis in subject matter can be found everywhere. It appears in Eustache Deschamps:

> Helas! On dit que je ne fais mès rien,
> Qui jadis fis mainte chose nouvelle;

La raison est que je n'ay pas merrien
Dont je fisse chose bonne ne belle.
(*Oeuvres complètes*, 6:191–92, no. 1204, ll. 1–4)

[Alas! People say that now I do nothing, I who once did
many new things; the reason is that I haven't the material
out of which to make good and beautiful things.]

We can find the same awareness in Jean Froissart, who exclaims in *Le
Joli Buisson de Jonece*:

Que porai-je de nouvel dire?   (L. 433)

[What new could I say?]

Martin Le Franc analyzed the crisis in his *Le Champion des dames*
(a work written between 1440 and 1442), and he suggested a possible
solution to the problem:

Item, on a fait tant de choses
Qu'on ne scet mais a quoy muser.
On a fait textes, or a gloses
Composer fault le temps user.
(MS, fol. 98, Fonds français 12476, Bibliothèque nationale,
Paris. This portion of the text is unpublished.)

[Similarly, «writers» made so many things that now «they»
hardly know what to amuse «themselves» with. «They» have
made texts; now we need to spend our time composing
glosses.]

The striking image of gleaning expressed the idea, which was a
painful one for men of the fourteenth century, that they followed after more illustrious predecessors. St. Bernard borrowed the image
from the Book of Ruth and used it to preach humility to monks:
"The great reapers are St. Augustine, St. Jerome, and St. Gregory, and
those who come after them should remain in the ranks of the poor
and the servants" (*Inédits bernardins dans un manuscrit d'Orval*,
quoted in Dom Jean Leclercq, *L'Amour des lettres*, 191; Misrahi translation, 249). During the thirteenth century, this image moved into
the secular domain, where it spoke of the difficulty of renewing literary subject matter. We find it in Huon de Méry's *Li Tournoiemenz*

Antecrist. The "harvesters" who had preceded Huon, and whom he names, were Chrétien de Troyes and Raoul de Houdenc. *Li Tournoiemenz* concludes with these words:

> Se j'ai trové aucun espi
> Apres la mein as mestiviers,
> Je l'ai glané molt volentiers.   (Ll. 3542–44)

> [If I have found an ear of grain left after the hand of the harvesters, I have gleaned it most willingly.]

The author of the *Avionnet* explains his working method in similar terms. He states in the epilogue that he has not "fait tout de [sa] teste" (l. 12) [done all with his head] but has compiled others' ideas:

> Je, qui suis des autres le pis,
> Après le grain, cuil les espis,
> Si comme fist Ruth la courtoise.   (2:382, ll. 19–21)

> [I, who am the worst of all, after the grain, I pick up the ears, as did the gentle Ruth.]

The same image appears in the work of Jean de Condé, whose case is exemplary because he was literally the son and heir of another poet, the minstrel Baudoin de Condé. Jean reflects on his legacy in *Le Dit dou levrier*:

> Car après ciaus cui les blés cuellent
> En awost, vont cil qui recuellent
> Ce qui lor ciet, et si l'assamblent,
> Et teil messonneur me resamblent,
> K'après lui vois pour recuellier
> Chou qui li remest au cuellier.
> (*Dits et contes,* vol. 2, ll. 55–60)

> [For after those who harvest the grain in August come those who pick up what falls from their hands and gather it together; and those gleaners resemble me, because I go behind him to gather up what remains to be picked.]

Another poet who inherited from her father, Christine de Pizan, used the same image to express her relationship to him. In the prologue to *L'Epistre Othea,* she repeats a topos of humility:

Car je n'ay sentement
En sens fondé, n'en ce cas ne ressemble
Mon bon pere, fors ainsi com l'en emble
Epis de blé en glenant en moissons,
Par mi ces champs et coste les buissons.　　(151, ll. 13–17)

[For I have no sentiment founded in reason, and in that I
do not resemble my good father, unless it is in the manner
of one who steals ears of grain by gleaning in harvest time
through the fields and by the bushes.]

Chaucer states in version F of the prologue of *The Legend of Good Women* (1386):

And I come after, glenyng here and there.
　　　　　　　　　　　　　　　　(*Works,* 484, l. 75)

On occasion, the image served a polemical purpose. Thus Guillaume de Digulleville used it to challenge the statement made at the beginning of *Le Roman de la Rose,* "La matiere est et bonne et neuve" [The matter is both good and new]. For Guillaume, a Cistercian monk, the subject matter of *Le Roman de la Rose* was neither good nor new. It was not good, because the portions concerning love had been dictated by an aging Venus. It was not new, for the entire work was not in fact by Jean de Meun. As Guillaume states in the second version of *Le Pèlerinage de vie humaine* (ca. 1355):

Il en embla en autrui champ.
　　　　　　　　(MS, fol. 52d, Fonds français 12466,
　　　　　　Bibliothèque nationale, Paris; quoted from Badel,
　　　　　　　Le Roman de la Rose au XIVe siècle, 369)

[He stole from another's field.]

We can follow the image of gleaning through the entire fifteenth century. For Georges Chastelain, Boccaccio provided the harvest that was being pilfered: "ne que moy, sy homme indoct et de sy gros engin, deusse aller jetter ma faucile en la messon ou sy glorieux homme avoit mis main" (*Le Temple de Bocace,* 195, ll. 11–12) [nor that I, a man of so little learning and of so dense a mind, should throw my sickle into the harvest to which such a famous man had put his hand].

For Guillaume Alexis, a monk in the Abbey of Lyre (in the diocese of Evreux) who wrote during the second half of the fifteenth century, the fields were Alain Chartier's and Michault Taillevent's:

> Or voys après eulx et amasse
> Les espiz du champ anobly.
> (*L'ABC des Doubles,* in *Oeuvres poétiques,* vol. 1, ll. 26–27)

[I go behind them and I gather the ears of grain from the ennobled field.]

Jean Lemaire de Belges says this of his historical works:

> Quoi que soit, j'ay cuidé fealement recueillir tout ce que les communs historiens de France et d'ailleurs, avoient laissé derriere au plus grand honneur de la nation Françoise. Et m'ha semblé que je faisoye comme font ceux qui amassent les menuz espis de blé, apres les moissonneurs: ou ceux qui gardent de perdre les raisins que les vendangeurs ont laissez derriere: laquelle chose est permise à chacun par droit divin et humain.
> (*Les Illustrations de Gaule et singularitez de Troye,* bk. 3, p. 468)

[I have always taken care, for the greater honor of the French nation, to gather faithfully all that the ordinary historians of France and elsewhere had left behind them. And it has seemed to me that I was acting like those who gather the little sprigs of wheat after the harvesters, or like those who take care that the grapes left behind by the harvesters not go to waste—as is permitted to everyone by divine and human law.]

Mathurin Régnier plays with the image in his third satire:

> Marquis, que doy-je faire en ceste incertitude?
> Dois-je, las de courir, me remettre à l'estude,
> Lire Homère, Aristote, et, disciple nouveau,
> Glaner ce que les Grecs ont de riche et de beau;
> Reste de ces moissons que Ronsard et des Portes
> Ont remporté du champ sur leurs espaules fortes,
> Qu'ils ont comme leur propre en leur grange entassé,
> Esgallant leurs honneurs aux honneurs du passé?
> (*Oeuvres complètes,* 26)

[Marquess, what must I do in this incertitude? Must I, weary of running, go back to studying, read Homer and Aristotle, and, a new disciple, glean what was rich and fine in the Greeks—the remainder of the harvests that Ronsard and Desportes bore off from the field on their burly shoulders, which they stocked in their graneries as their own, equaling their honors to those of the past?]

Although the gleaning image was by far the most frequent, there were other metaphors to express the same notion. In *Le Livre de la mutacion de fortune,* Christine de Pizan deplored having kept only "paillettes" (bk. 1, chap. 6) [wisps of straw] from her father's treasures, and in *L'Epistre Othea* she speaks of "mietes cheans de haulte table" (prologue, l. 18) [crumbs falling from the high table], another biblical image and one that follows the gleaning image in the same passage. Or the metaphor could be culinary. In his *Voir-Dit,* Guillaume de Machaut describes competing with another poet to write a double ballade:

> .T. fist devant, plus n'en escript;
> Et le mieus et le plus qu'il pot,
> Print toute la gresse du pot,
> Si qu'il ot assez l'aventage
> De faire millour son potage.   (Ll. 6738–42)

> [T. began; he wrote no more; and, as best he could and as much, he skimmed all the grease from the pot; thus he had a real advantage for making his soup better.]

The feeling that subject matter was scarce engendered reflection on the act of writing itself and on the forms that writing should take in a situation of scarcity. An aesthetic of collecting treasures and of the reuse of materials accompanied the crisis of subject matter.

The aesthetic of the collection of treasures was made concrete in the image of the coffer or strongbox. As in Guillaume de Machaut's *Voir-Dit,* a *coffre* might be used to store portraits, the source material for creation whose loss the poet mourns. It might contain poems—in the case of Jean Froissart in *La Prison amoureuse,* poetic texts that he had completed. Froissart tells us he even enjoyed making *coffrets*:

Car moult volentiers m'ensonnie
A passer le tamps sur tel cose.   (Ll. 1251–52)

[For I spend time willingly on such things.]

Froissart presents this manual activity as a true image of his poetic composition. He also describes putting lyrics—in one instance, a virelay—in such a coffer:

Je le mis en une laiette
Que j'avoie proprement fete
De danemarce bien ounie.   (Ll. 1248–50)

[I put it in a little box that I had made myself out of highly polished Danish wood.]

He did the same with some ballades:

J'avoie adont de cuir bouli
Un coffinet bel et poli,
Qu'estoit longés et estrois,
Ou les balades toutes trois
Mis, car ensi user soloie.   (Ll. 2114–18)

[At the time I had a little coffer made out of one piece of fine boiled leather; it was fairly long and narrow, and I put the three ballades in it, as was my custom.]

Storing poems in a coffer plays on the two notions of deferral and delegation; poetry operates at a distance rather than directly, in the poet's presence. Guillaume de Machaut took a first step in that direction. In *La Fonteinne amoureuse* the poet overhears a lover's poetic lament through a wall. His reaction (a reflex that was to become more typical in the fourteenth century) was to note down that "dolereuse complainte" (l. 214) to preserve it. Guillaume de Machaut insists on this scribal activity:

Si que je pris mon escriptoire,
Qui est entaillie d'ivoire,
Et tous mes outils pour escrire
La complainte qu'i voloit dire.

(*Oeuvres,* vol. 3, ll. 229–32)

[And so I took up my writing desk, which is worked with ivory, and all my writing instruments in order to record the complaint that he intended to utter (Palmer translation, 101).]

When the prince later asked the poet to write "ou lay ou complainte" (l. 1504) [a lay or complaint] about his unhappiness, the poet was able to respond immediately by producing a transcription of what the prince himself had composed the evening before and the poet had noted down:

> Ma main mis a ma gibessiere,
> S'ataingni sa complainte entiere
> Et dis: "Sire, vostre requeste,
> Tenez: vesla ci toute preste."   (Ll. 1517–20)

[I put my hand to my wallet, took out all of his complaint, and said, "Lord, take what you've requested; here it is, at once" (Palmer translation, 171).]

Here the wallet or game bag is the first substitute for the coffer, but it is still a figure that refers to chivalric values by alluding to the hunt. Moreover, Guillaume's scenario emphasizes the idea of gift and countergift. The fact that he notes down the poem and stores it away is not a deliberate move but the result of a happy chance; he simply gives back to the prince the poem that is rightfully his. In this vision of the world and of the role of the various "estates" of society, the prince is the prime lover. In *La Fonteinne amoureuse,* Guillaume de Machaut insists on the respective roles of the knight and the clerk:

> Car je vueil tesmongnier et dire
> Que chevaliers acouardis
> Et clers qui vuet estre hardis
> Ne valent plein mon pong de paille
> En fait d'armes ou en bataille,
> Car chascuns fait contre droiture;
> Dont, s'ils font bien, c'est aventure.   (Ll. 132–38)

[For I intend to testify and state that a cowardly knight and a clerk who would be brave aren't worth my hand full of

straw in a passage of arms or battle, for each is acting against
what is right; and so, if they do well, it's luck (Palmer translation, 97).]

The conditions of the exchange between the poet and the prince
evolved between Guillaume de Machaut and Jean Froissart. In *La
Fonteinne amoureuse,* Guillaume de Machaut presents Jean de Berry
as a prince who knew how to be generous with his gifts and to make
wealth circulate, as his role demanded. A passage near the beginning
of the work makes this notion explicit. The prince had received a pal-
frey, a sparrow-hawk, and a little dog from one of his neighbors:

> Le don prisa moult hautement
> Et le reçut courtoisement
> En disant: "Vesci riche don.
> Bien est dignes de guerredon."   (Ll. 1141–44)

> [He valued the gift very highly, receiving it politely and say-
> ing: "What a rich present! This certainly deserves recom-
> pense" (Palmer translation, 151).]

The prince thanks the messenger and gives him fifteen florins. Almost immediately ("tout en l'eure"; l. 1148) he sends "le chien, l'oisel,
la haguenee" (l. 1149) [the dog, the bird, the horse (Palmer translation, 151)] to a lady. At the beginning of *La Prison amoureuse,* Jean
Froissart praises largesse:

> Certes, c'est une bonne tece
> Que uns grans sires puet avoir
> D'estre larges de son avoir.   (Ll. 54–56)

> [Certainly it is a good quality that a great lord may have to
> be generous with his wealth.]

The words *dons* and *guerredons* (gifts; rewards) reappear later in
the same text (ll. 77–78), where the prince who provides an example
of generosity—Jean de Luxembourg—embodies traditional chivalric
virtues. But whereas that prince was the protector of Guillaume de
Machaut, Jean Froissart, who was only nine years old when Jean de
Luxembourg died at Crécy, never enjoyed his protection. Thus the

generosity incarnate in the king of Bohemia was just a memory for Froissart. The statements that he attributes to the king are significant:

> Tous li avoirs qui est en Bruges
> Repus en coffres et un huges
> Ne m'euïst valu une pomme,
> Se n'euïssent esté chil homme
> Qui m'ont a mon besoing servi.   (Ll. 85–89)

[All the wealth that is in Bruges, hidden in coffers or hutches, would have done me no good without the men who served me when I needed them.]

But why, if money was supposed to flow out of coffers, should poems be put into them? Precisely because the times called for savings. Largesse was praised because it was no longer practiced, as satirical texts repeated tirelessly. Eustache Deschamps gives ample confirmation. If the great lords and high prelates were storing up wealth, what could the poet put aside? Money? Certainly not in Froissart's case. He speaks of his inability to save money in *Le Dit dou florin,* where the image of the prison is trenchant. A purse was a prison that, no matter how well "pourveüe" (l. 105) [furnished], could not hold its coins:

> J'avoie acheté en ce jour
> Une boursette trois deniers
> Et la, comme mes prisonniers,
> Les quarante frans encloÿ.
>
> . . . .
>
> Or avoi je mis mon avoir
> Et la boursette, tres le soir,
> En une aultre bourse plus grans.
> Quant je cuidai trouver mes frans,
> Certes je ne trouvais riensnee.
> ("*Dits*" et "*Débats,*" ll. 396–99; 403–7)

[I had bought, that very day, a little purse for three pennies, and there, like my prisoners, I shut up the forty francs. . . . Toward evening I put my store and the little purse into another bigger purse. When I went to find my francs, in truth, I found nothing at all.]

Putting one's purse into another purse, and so on ad infinitum, was no way to avoid loss. If Froissart was good at getting rid of money ("argent desfaire"), he was less good at making it again ("refaire") or putting it together, bit by bit ("rapiecier ne remettre ensamble"), as he tells us in the opening lines of the same text (ll. 1–3). But *refaire, rapiécer,* and *remettre ensemble* are precisely what writing does. Since gift and countergift—*spartio*—and largesse were dead, what the poet could accumulate and, when need be, recycle on the market was poetry.

A notable change took place between the coffers and coffins of the twelfth century, which held warm, still palpitating bodies (the nightingale in the *Laustic* of Marie de France, a symbolic entombment of the living voice, or the lady buried alive in the *Cligès* of Chrétien de Troyes), and the *coffins* of the fourteenth century that held a body of poems—ballades that the poet could resuscitate when the right moment came.

Storing up treasures implied a theory of later use. Christine de Pizan gives an explicit description of how she went about this in *Le Livre des fais et bonnes meurs du sage roy Charles V.* Responding to potential criticism, she states:

> Ilz pourroient dire: "Ceste femme-cy ne dit mie de soy ce que elle explique en son livre, ains fait son traittié par procès de ce que autres auteurs on[t] dit à la lettre"; de laquel chose à ceulz je puis responde que tout ainsi comme l'ovrier de architeture ou maçonnage n'a mie fait les pierres et les estoffes, dont il bastist et ediffie le chastel ou maison, qu'il tent à perfaire et où il labeure, non obstant assemble les matieres ensemble, chascune où elle doit servir, selon la fin de l'entencion où il tent, aussi les brodeurs, qui font diverses divises, selon la soubtivité de leur ymaginacion, sanz faulte ne firent mie les soyes, l'or, ne les matieres, et ainsi d'aultres ouvrages, tout ainsi vrayement n'ay je mie fait toutes les matieres, de quoy le traittié de ma compilacion est composé; il me souffist seulement que les sache appliquer à propos, si que bien puissent servir à la fin de l'ymaginacion, à laquelle je tends à perfaire.
>
> (1:190–91)

[They can say: "That woman does not draw out of herself what she exposes in her book; quite to the contrary, she composes her treatise by following word for word what other authors say." I can answer them thus: just as a worker in architecture or masonry has not made the stones and the materials with which he builds and edifies the castle or the house that he strives to complete and for which he labors, and in spite of that, he puts together the materials, each in its place according to its purpose; and just as embroiderers, who vary their designs according to the subtlety of their imagination, in no case make the silk threads, the gold, or the other materials—and so on for other sorts of work—so, in truth, I have not made all the materials of which my compilation is made. It is enough that I know how to apply them appropriately to serve my purpose.]

Borrowing became a compositional technique, whether authors used extracts from the works of earlier writers or—and this was new —explicitly reused their own writings. It was not borrowing that was reprehensible but concealing the practice. There is a measurable difference between this theory of creative composition in Christine de Pizan and the theory of imitation in Petrarch. In a letter to Boccaccio, Petrarch speaks of reutilization in terms of an "air" of resemblance: "That similarity must not be like the image to its original in painting, where the greater the similarity, the greater the praise for the artist, but rather like that of a son to his father. . . . Thus we may appropriate another's ideas as well as his coloring, but we must abstain from his actual words" (Petrarch, *Lettres de François Pétrarque à Jean Boccace,* bk. 23, letter 19, p. 46; quoted from *Letters on Familiar Matters,* Bernardo translation, 3:301–2).

This was a theory of creative transformation, not a theory of composition. Petrarch stressed style over form. Starting from the same fondness for books that Christine displayed, Petrarch had already moved on to another aesthetic.

The sentiment of a crisis in materials engendered reflection on the very ways in which literary materials were produced and on the origins of the work of literature. This led to an exploration that took place on several levels—ontological, phenomenological, mythic, and historical.

The Thickets and Chaos of Origins

Language taught that *matter* was related to *mother*. Isidore of
Seville stated as much: "Mater dicitur quod exinde efficiatur aliquid.
Mater enim quasi materia. Nam causa pater est" (*Etymologiarum*, bk.
9, chap. 5, sec. 6) [*Mother* comes from having something born of her.
Mater is, in effect, like *materia*. For it is the father who is the cause].
Reflection oscillated between the thing (*chose*) and the cause; between
materia/*mater* and the *causa* that was the paternal form. Dame Opinion, the shadowy creature who converses with Christine de Pizan in
L'Avision Christine, teaches this in Aristotelian terms: "Et toutefois, de
matiere premierement, comme de son principe, chascune chose est
faitte, car la matiere precede la fourmacion. Et aussi la matiere premierement, non pas accidentelment est le suppost des fourmes, par
quoy encore appert qu'elle soit vray principe. Il s'ensuit que matere soit
principe des choses" (*Lavision-Christine*, 117) [Yet everything is made
first from matter as from its principle because matter precedes formation. Matter is also principally (not accidentally) the medium of forms,
by which it again appears that it must be the true principle. There-
fore, matter must be the origin of things (McLeod translation, 65)].

How did the Middle Ages imagine matter? As Christine de Pizan
presented it in the beginning of her *Avision*, matter, in its primal in-
division, was the unity of origins, the primordial chaos:

> Le grand ymage, dont a son commencement ce dit livre parle,
> pour tout le monde puet estre pris; c'est asavoir ciel, terre et
> abeisme. Son nom qu'escript en son front portoit, c'est assavoir
> *Chaoz*, puet estre entendu que a son commencement les pouetes
> anciens nommerent la masse que Dieu fourma, dont il trey ciel et
> terre et toutes choses, *chaos*, qui est a dire confusion, qui encore as-
> sez est au monde. Les .ii. conduis qu'il avoit par ou peüz estoit et
> purgiéz se puet entendre la naissance de toutes corporelles choses,
> et aussi la mort de toute creature vive.
>
> ("Glose sur la premiere partie de ce present volume,"
> in *L'Advision Christine*, 1–2)

[The large figure discussed at the beginning of the book can be
taken for the whole world, or heaven, earth, and the abyss. His

name, which he carried on his forehead, "chaos," can be interpreted that at its beginning, the ancient poets named the mass that
God formed and from which he made heaven, earth, and all
things, "chaos," or confusion, which still prevails in the world. His
two conduits through which he was fed and purged can be understood as the birth of all corporeal things and also as the death of
all living creatures (McLeod translation, 3).]

That chaos might be seen as a forest, the *materia prima* or the *hylè*
of the Greeks. This was the dark wood in which Dante wandered at
the beginning of *The Divine Comedy* (*Inferno*, canto 1, ll. 4–5), the
"selva selvaggia e aspra e forte" [rough and stubborn forest] that he
found "quanto a dir . . . cosa dura" [hard to speak of (Sayers translation, 71)]. It was the *silve* that Christine de Pizan spoke of in *Le
Chemin de long estude* (l. 1131), the shadowy, formless depths that were
like infancy. Matter, as it referred to origins, evoked what was most
elementary, and the forest was its metaphorical paradigm. Matter was
whatever was in the raw state, rough, untreated, rudimentary. It was
like earth (one of its figures) in that it was the opposite of everything
poli (polished) and *policé* (disciplined, civilized), the opposite of art's
subtlety and of all that was second. The *Ovide moralisé,* following
Ovid himself,[1] offers this definition:

> Ce n'est fors un moncel de forme,
> Sans art, sans devise et sans forme,
> Ou toute estoit en discordance
> Jointe des choses la semance.   (Vol. 1, bk. 1, ll. 155–58)

[It is merely a heap of shapes without art, without distinction, and without form, in which all the seed of things was
brought together without order.]

Concordia discors—but given that "matter" was "mother," although it might be rough it was round; it might not be polished or
smooth, but it was soft and warm. And since matter preceded division, the carving out of the sign, it was noncontradictory. Finally, the

---

1. Ovid says *rudis indigestaque moles* (rough, unordered mass, but also "undigested").

mother—like the forest—might frighten, terrify, and engulf, but she also soothed, lulled, and calmed.

The matter of medieval literature was the *mesrien*—the wood, the construction material—on which poets reflected. "De vieil mesrien neufve maison" [A new house from old wood] ran the proverb repeated by Jean de Bueil in *Le Jouvencel*. The proverb reappears in the *Adevineaux amoureux* in the form of a riddle:

> *Demande*
> Comment feroit on de trois vielz deux nouveaulz?
> *Response*
> Tout ainsi qu'en toute saison
> Se fait de vielz boiz noeufve maison,
> Fait on bien par commun usage
> De deux vielz culz noeuf mariage.
>
> (Demande 389, pp. 101–2)

[Question: How can one turn three old ones «a possible pun on *vieux* and *vits*?» into two new ones? Answer: Just as, in all seasons, one makes a new house out of old wood, common wisdom says that two old bodies make a new marriage.]

The Middle Ages used this proverb optimistically, as an image for rewriting. For instance, Jean Regnier, rewriting a rondeau of Alain Chartier's, declares in his *Fortunes et adversitez*:

> Je vueil estre le charpentier
> Ou masson, qui est de mestier,
> Qui font souvent par leur raison
> De vieil mesrien neufve maison.   (Ll. 4391–94)

[I want to be the carpenter or mason whose skills are needed, and who, by their intelligence, often make a new house out of old materials.]

The image could also be used pessimistically, to show the fragility of youth and of novelty. When this was done, *mesrien* rhymed resoundingly with *rien*. Thus Michault Taillevent, who served Philippe le Bon, wrote in *Le Passe Temps*:

> Et a celle heure me sembloit
> Qu'il ne me fauldroit jamais rien:
> De maison neufve viel mairien.   (136, stanza 7, ll. 47–49)

[And at the time, it seemed to me that I would never lack for anything: for a new house, old materials.]

Both a marriage and literature might lack the wood—the *mesrien* (*merrien; mairien*)—needed for construction, as we have seen with Eustache Deschamps. And the *mesrien* that echoed *rien,* as a thing or as real nothingness, true void, was the very matter of medieval literature in its ambivalence and its nonsegmentation. It was the forest, echoing and reechoing, in which the question of identity was posed and resolved (or not resolved), along with the question of *être fors*—the sonic inverse of *forest*—that is, of being outside the primal matrix. A path wound from the chivalric forest of the adventure romances to internal forests of tenebrous thought, long expectant waits, and wearisome gloom. It led to the "forest de Longue Pensee" of Richard de Fournival, to the "gaste forest de Longue Actente" written in the wake of Alan Chartier's *La Belle Dame sans mercy,* to the "forest de Longue Actente" and the "forest d'Ennuyeuse Tristesse" of Charles d'Orléans. In such a forest, the poet's task was to distinguish the tree, the staff, the stick, to extract the pith, trace the straight line, find the element of rectitude that would enable him to trace his route or just to grope his way, perhaps even to turn raw wood into literature, *liber* into *livre.* The ballade of Charles d'Orléans, "En la Forest d'Ennuyeuse Tristesse," ends with this envoi:

> Aveugle suy, ne sçay ou aler doye;
> De mon baston, affin que ne forvoye,
> Je vois tastant mon chemin ça et la;
> C'est grant pitié qu'il couvient que je soye
> L'omme esgaré qui ne scet ou il va!
>   (*Poésies,* vol. 1, ballade 63, ll. 25–29)

[I am blind, and know not where I should go; with my stick, lest I wander from the path, I go tapping out my way

here and there; it is great pity that I must be the lost man
that knows not where he is going (Purcell translation, 69).]

The Long Road of Study

Thing/cause, matter/form, feminine principle/masculine principle—it is interesting to see how those philosophical categories were
applied in literary theory. The pair matter/form became linked in literary aesthetics to refer to the two first steps in rhetoric: *inventio* and
dispositio. Guillaume de Machaut inverted the order of the terms—a
sure sign of the crisis in the literary material under analysis. For him,
form came first and was given by Nature; matter was given by Love.
The lady replaced the mother. This view had interesting results. According to the division of social roles put into operation by Guillaume de Machaut (who followed tradition here), arms and love were
the province of the prince, and writing the domain of the clerk. In
other words, in Guillaume's poetics, the prince ruled in the realm of
matter, the clerk in the realm of form.

This fitted perfectly into the scheme of relations between the poet
and his patron, since the poet received commands and treated topics
dictated to him. But by linking the prince to matter, Guillaume
made him into a sort of female figure akin to the poet's lady. In fact,
in Provence the term *midons,* a derivative of *mon seigneur* (my lord)
and masculine in gender, was applied to the lady. In a parallel movement, Guillaume granted to the poet the virile figure who gives form
to the matter of female seed in the generative act (a persistent
metaphor for literary creation). This was what medical theory derived from reading and rereading Aristotle's *De generatione* throughout the Middle Ages. In Guillaume's *La Fonteinne amoureuse* the
prince laments, wails, and weeps, thus giving amorous matter to the
poet on the other side of the wall who transcribes, writes, and in-
scribes those laments, working on his "escriptoire . . . entaillie
d'ivoire" (*Oeuvres,* vol. 3, ll. 229–30) [writing desk . . . worked with
ivory (Palmer translation, 101)].

The situation was actually even more complex. Both the prince and the poet were feminized. The prince goes to sleep on the poet's lap:

> Son bras et son chef mist sor mi
> Et moult doucement s'endormi
> Droitement enmi mon giron. (Ll. 1543–45)

[He leaned his arm and head on me and very softly fell asleep right in my lap (Palmer translation, 171).]

The two men take the same pose as the poet and his lady in the *Voir-Dit.* In the episode of the meeting under the cherry tree and the stolen kiss, Guillaume says:

> Mais sur mon giron s'enclina
> La belle, qui douceur fine a. (Ll. 2257–58)

[But the beautiful lady of exquisite sweetness leaned over onto my lap.]

When the poet and his lady are tucked into bed in a cozy, closed-in bedchamber, we see the earlier scene in the orchard transposed (one might almost say, translated, as for a relic) to the bedroom:

> Et la ma dame s'endormi,
> Tousdis l'un de ses bras sur mi. (Ll. 3467–68)

[And there my lady went to sleep, still with one of her arms on me.]

Here, an intimate outdoor scene moves indoors to a closeted interior.

The poet is also feminized, however, and his actions are part maternal, part virginal. Thus in *La Fonteinne amoureuse,* he covers the prince with his cloak:

> Mais einsois de mon mantelet
> Le couvri pour le ventelet
> Qui ventoit. (*Oeuvres,* vol. 3, ll. 1555–57)

[But first I covered him with my cloak because of the breeze which then was blowing (Palmer translation, 173).]

The poet, like the virgin required to capture a unicorn, takes a sleeping figure on his lap. Pierre de Beauvais writes in *Le Bestiaire*: "Si tost

com l'unicorne le [la meschine virge] voit, ele s'endort en son giron.
Ainsi faitierement est prise des veneors et menee aus roiaus palés.
Tout autresi Nostre Sires Jehsu Criz, esperitueus unicornes, decendi
en la Virge et par la char que vesti pour nos fu pris des juis" (art. 15,
pp. 71–72) [As soon as the unicorn sees the virgin, it goes to sleep in
her lap. This is how, by ruse, it is captured by the hunters and taken
to the royal palace. In the same manner, Our Lord Jesus Christ, spiritual unicorn, descended into the womb of the Virgin, and by the
flesh that he took on for us was captured by the Jews].

Richard de Fournival, in his *Bestiaire d'amours,* specifies that the
unicorn was captured thanks to its sense of smell: "Et par le flairier
meïsme fui je pris, ausi com li unicornes ki s'endort au douc[h] flair
de la virginité a la damoisele. . . . Si ke li sage veneor ki se nature
seivent metent une pucele en son trespas, et il s'endort en son geron"
(*Il Bestiario d'amore,* 56, ll. 13–14, 19–21) [I was captured also by smell,
like the unicorn, which falls asleep at the sweet smell of maidenhood.
. . . Consequently, the clever hunters who know its nature put a
maiden in its path, and it falls asleep in her lap (Beer translation, 15)].

The poet, as virgin and mother, likens himself to Mary. The scene of
going to sleep becomes an Annunciation, but a pagan Annunciation.
Venus appears to *aombrer* (provide shade for) the sleeping pair. She fe-
cundates the work in a mythological discourse addressed to the poet:

> Car Venus parla longuement
> De la pomme a moy seulement.
>   (*La Fonteinne amoureuse,* in *Oeuvres,* vol. 3, ll. 2637–38)
>
> [But Venus spoke a long time about the apple to me alone
> (Palmer translation, 229).]

Venus plants the seed of loving comfort in the prince's heart. Similarly, in the *Voir-Dit,* Venus descends in a "nue obscure" [dark cloud]
that serves the lovers as "ciel et couverture" (ll. 3788–89) [sky and cov-
ering]. Their *aombrement* lasts the time it takes to compose a *chanson
baladée* (ll. 3794–97). The poet asks his lady:

> Avez vous bien apperceü
> La deesse que j'ai veü?

.   .   .   .
Comment elle nous aombra
De sa nue, qui douce ombre ha?   (Ll. 3857–58, 3861–62)

[Did you see the goddess I saw? . . . How she covered us
with her sweet-shading cloud?]

We have moved from the physical shade of the cherry tree to an
aombrement by Venus that echoes the descent of the Holy Spirit into
the womb of the Virgin. All borderlines—sexual, cultural, and religious—have been blurred, and only the *chanson baladée* (that is, poetry) can express the unutterable truth of the thing.

The scenario of creation and incarnation can be found in a quite
different guise in Christine de Pizan. Christine depicts the genesis of
her works in a scene in which we find her leafing through a book,
reading, in the precise pose shown by the illuminators in the illustration at the head of the first page. Her *Chemin de long estude* begins,
"Si cerchay un livre ou deux" (l. 177) [I looked for a book or two]; *Le
Livre de la cité des dames* begins with a similar notion: "Et comme
adonc en celle entente je cerchasce entour moy d'aucun petit livret"
(616) [With this in mind, I searched for some small book (Richards
translation, 3)]. That scene can be interpreted, on a first level, as an
attempt to depict a familiarity with books in order to reflect the labor
of *translatio* that Christine was performing on her models, whether
negative models, such as the *Lamentations* of Matheolus (in *La Cité
des dames*), or positive ones, such as Boethius's *De consolatione
philosophiae* (at the beginning of *Le Chemin de long estude*).

The reading scene—a device for launching the narration and a fable illustrating intertextuality—is doubled, in *La Cité des dames*, by
another panel of the diptych, which balances the first, giving it its
second meaning and its full depth, since Christine tells us that this is
how poets should be read. That second scene is an Annunciation:
"En celle dollente penssee ainsi que j'estoye, la teste baissiee comme
personne honteuse, les yeulx plains de larmes, tenant ma main soubz
ma joe acoudee sur le pommel de ma chayere, soubdainement sus
mon giron vy descendre un ray de lumiere si comme se le soleil fust"

(621–22) [So occupied with these painful thoughts, my head bowed in shame, my eyes filled with tears, leaning on the pommel of my chair's armrest «we recognize the attitude typical of melancholy», I suddenly saw a ray of light fall on my lap, as though it were the sun (Richards translation, 6)].

Although the three poets strike an identical attitude of affliction, Christine is not merely reformulating the scene in which Philosophy appears to Boethius, which Guillaume de Machaut had rewritten in *Le Remede de fortune* as the appearance of Hope. She is also playing with the sacred. With humble pride, she is putting herself in the place of the Virgin, who is often depicted in Annunciation scenes with a book (rather, with "the Book") in her hand. Christine receives in her *giron*—the word is fundamental, as the ambiguity of lap and womb announces the coming maternity—a light that comes from on high. Reason, the daughter of God (and Christine takes pains to stress that point in order to guarantee the orthodoxy of her thought) descends to her, accompanied by Rectitude and Justice. The Annunciation scene becomes for the poet a scene of inspiration; the engendering of the book substitutes for the engendering of Christ. This was a new conception of the writer and his or her new pride.

Le Dit de la Rose, written in 1402, two years before *La Cité des dames,* contains a prefiguration of that scene. Love visits his loyal friends who have gathered together to talk of love and of poetry (an allusion to the founding of the Ordre de la Rose):

> Car alors seurvint tout a point,
> Non obstant les portes barrées
> Et les fenestres bien sarrées,
> Une dame de grant noblesse
> Qui s'appela dame et deesse
> De Loyauté, et trop belle yere.
> La descendi a grant lumiere
> Si que toute en resplent la sale.
>
> (*Oeuvres poétiques,* vol. 2, ll. 86–93)

[Just then there came, in spite of barred doors and carefully closed windows «I might note that Christ appeared to his

disciples in spite of similar obstacles», a most noble lady
who told us she was the lady and goddess of Loyalty, and
she was truly beautiful. She descended with a great light,
such that the entire room was illuminated.]

In the joining of these two scenes, the reading scene and the annunciation scene, Christine presents her model for her literary creation, its dual sources, sacred and profane; her dual orientation in the
labor of the clerk and the inspiration of the poet and her relationship
to tradition and to God. Pagan mythology and Christian imagery are
mixed in this episode from *Le Dit de la Rose.* Loyalty has been sent by
the god of love and comes surrounded by nymphs (l. 99) who seem
like "angelz" (l. 247). They seem to come from Paradise and to be
messengers from God. Loyalty is not Venus, and the roses she brings
are not the golden apple of the judgment of Paris or the apple of
Adam and Eve's fall and of original sin. Concord has replaced dis-
cord. Christine de Pizan's imagery is Christian, but it is grafted onto
ancient models. The work of literature is produced by an "elect" person covered by the shadow of God. The literary work is a true birth,
a maternity. Images of maternity are of capital importance in Christine's work. She makes them explicit in *L'Avision.* Nature enjoins her
servant:

> Ou temps que tu portoies les enfans en ton ventre, grant douleur
> a l'enfanter sentoies. Or vueil que de toy naiscent nouveaulx vo-
> lumes lesquieulx, le temps a venir et perpetuelment au monde pre-
> senteront ta memoire devant les princes et par lumiers en toutes
> places lesquieulx en joye et delit tu enfanteras de te memoire non
> obstant le labour et travail. Lequel, tout ainsi comme la femme qui
> a enfanté, si tost que ot le cry de l'enfant, oublie son mal, oubliera
> le travail du labour oyant la voix de tes volumes. (*Lavision-Chris-
> tine,* 163–64)

[When you carried children in your womb, you experienced great
pain in order to give birth. Now I want new books brought forth
from you which will present your memory before the worldly
princes in the future and keep it always and everywhere bright;
these you will deliver from your memory in joy and pleasure
notwithstanding the pain and labor. Just as the woman who has

given birth to a child forgets her pain as soon as she hears the cry of the infant, so will you forget the pain of labor in hearing the voice of your books (McLeod translation, 119).]

The maternity of the Virgin also touched a chord in Christine. She writes in *Les XV joyes Nostre Dame*:

> Doulce dame, vueilles pitié avoir
> De mon ame pour ycelle leesce
> Que tu eus quant en ton ventre mouvoir
> Le Filz de Dieu sentis plein de sagece.
>
> (*Oeuvres poétiques*, 3:12, ll. 13–16)

> [Sweet lady, deign to take pity on my soul, in the name of the joy that you had when you felt the son of God, full of wisdom, moving in your womb.])

The physical experience of childbirth that Christine herself had undergone made her optimistic regarding her literary progeny. In the prologue to *L'Epistre Othea*, in the line immediately preceding the topos of humility in which she speaks of herself gleaning in her father's field, she argues that her work merits consideration, "car moult en est la matiere nouvelle" (prologue, l. 11) [for so much is the matter herein new]. This is a repetition (a century later and not without malice) of the triumphant affirmation of novelty in *Le Roman de la Rose*.

This same cannot be said of Guillaume de Machaut. For him, the birth of a literary work was a birth without a mother. The fables that he retells in the *Voir-Dit*—for example, the birth of Erichthonius, engendered solely of the seed of Vulcan stricken with desire for Pallas Athena, and the birth of Aesculapius, extracted from the dead body of his mother—are proof enough of that.[2]

Virgin or Poet: The Model of the Incarnation

The Incarnation, the Word made flesh, marked a rift. It instituted a "before" and an "after," both in the history of divine creation and

---

2. See the analysis in Jacqueline Cerquiglini, *"Un Engin si soutil": Guillaume de Machaut et l'écriture au XIVe siècle*, 152–55.

in that of literary creation. Alain Chartier announced this in *Le Livre de l'Esperance,* using the medieval terminology for the theory of pre-figuration:

> Sy est l'embuche desclose,
> Le signe cede a la chose. (Poésie 13, ll. 33–34)

> [What was hidden is revealed; the sign gives way to the thing.]

The representation of literary creation in the Middle Ages adopted the model of the Incarnation because it did not dare use the one of the creation of the world. The poet did not yet hazard taking the place of God, but he (or she) did accept to take—and even demand —a virgin's place. Literary imagination had two choices. The first involved finding a concrete image for literary matter, usually as a secret enclosed in the womb of a virgin, huddled on the lap of a poet, or shut up within the space of a book—for the book was a place in the Middle Ages: one read *in* (*en*) a book. This was the Incarnation model; there was a mystery of love in the appearance of all matter. But an image was needed for the production of the work itself. The model for this was fabrication, the masculine model of the stamp, the chisel, or the forge. The text of *La Guerre de Metz en 1324* opens with these "trenchant" lines:

> Pour eschevir mirancolie
> Qui m'ait esteit souvent contraire,
> Une matiere ai entaillie
> Dont je volra plusieurs vers faire. (Stanza 1)

> [To flee melancholy, which often was against me, I have cut into a subject on which I would like to make several stanzas.]

These models are illustrated and treated ironically in *Le Traité de Geta et d'Amphitrion* by Eustache Deschamps, a *translatio* of the *Geta* of Vital de Blois, written between 1150 and 1160, which was in turn based on the *Amphitruo* of Plautus. Eustache Deschamps's text offers several levels of parody. He presents Jupiter and his son Archas (in Plautus, Mercury) taking on human form as a mock incarnation:

Tant est es dieux humilité
Qu'ilz prindrent la mortalité
Et devindrent, ou bel ou let,
L'un seigneur, et l'autre varlet;
Le fil varlet, seigneur le pere,
Si com je truis en la matere.

(Oeuvres complètes, 8:213, no. 1494, ll. 57–62)

[So much humility was there in the gods that they took on
the appearance of mortals and became, handsome or ugly,
the one lord, the other servant; the son, the servant, the father, the lord, just as I find it in the source.]

The love that was the motivation for this incarnation is ignoble—
un amour de ribaud (the love of a debauchee), the text tells us. Eustache Deschamps carries his desacralization one step further when
the god inhabiting the servant, Geta (who is a thief), speaks of his
criminal activities:

Une huche ouvry sans froissier
N'a gueres.   (Ll. 801–2)

[I opened a cupboard without breaking it; there was no
time.]

The mystery of the incarnation, of the light that passes through glass
without breaking it, is transposed into the domain of stealth bur-
glary, entry by ruse, counterfeit, and a skeleton key (*sousclave*). Technological prowess took the place of miracle.

Similarly, one might read the entrance of Christine de Pizan's real-
life mother at the end of *Le Chemin de long estude* as a mock annunciation. When the mother appears, like an all too secular *deus ex
machina,* her arrival snaps her daughter out of her dream and brings
her back down to earth:

Ja estoie bas desjuchee,
Ce me sembloit, quant fus huchee
De la mere qui me porta,
Qu'a l'uis de ma chambre hurta
Qui de tant gesir s'esmerveille,
Car tart estoit, et je m'esveille.   (Ll. 6387–92)

[I had already come down «the Sibyl's ladder», it seems to me, when I was called by the mother who bore me. Indeed, she rapped on my door, astonished to see me stay in bed so long, for it was late, and I awoke.]

The place of this episode in the economy of the text makes its parodic intent clear, and it underlines Christine's low opinion of her mother's qualifications where learning was concerned. In this passage, the mother represents common opinion at its most aleatory, as dependant on *doxa* (opinion), and as contrary to reason and right thinking. Christine (following Aristotle and St. Thomas here) contrasts the certitude of opinion to the certitude of knowledge and of faith. Droiture (Rectitude) proclaims that opinion must be rejected, which implies the distancing of the person in whom opinion is incarnate, here Christine's birth mother, who would prefer to see her daughter busy herself with needlework and spinning—*fillasses*—as Christine tells us in *Le Livre de la cité des dames* (875). This is why Christine eliminates her real mother from her genealogy and puts Nature in her place in *Le Livre de la mutacion de fortune*.

In *Le Traité de Geta et d'Amphitrion*, Eustache Deschamps offers a mimed false birth. Geta, the servant-logician who represents form, uses a pitchfork to get Birrea, a lazy servant who represents matter, to come out of the cave (something like a regression to the womb) in which he has taken refuge:

> Lors de sa fourche fiert un pou
> En la caverne droit au trou;
> Semblant fait de bouter avant,
> Et met son chaperon devant.
> (*Oeuvres complètes*, 8:225, no. 1494, ll. 423–26)

[Then, with his forked stick, he casts about a bit in the middle of the hole of the cavern; he makes as if to thrust his stick deeper, then puts his hat at the mouth of the cave.]

This scene of copulation and birth uses hunting terms. The word *chaperon* functions like what hunters call a *bourse* (a sack to trap small animals such as rabbits). But the text contains a real birth—that of

Hercules, fathered by Jupiter—concealed in the tracery of a tapestry.
Eustache Deschamps gives this description of Alcmena:

> Lors fist les liz parer de soye,
> Les champbres tendre de draps d'or;
> De haulte liche y ot encore
> Draps faiz de l'istoire de Troye,
> Mainte bataille et mainte proye
> Des faiz d'Erculès et Jason.   (Ll. 68–73)

> [Then she had the beds made with silk and had cloth of
> gold hung about. There were also high-warp tapestries bear-
> ing the story of Troy and showing the many battles and
> booties of the deeds of Hercules and Jason.]

The bedroom, decorated with "tapis d'oeuvre sarrasinoise" (l. 75)
[rugs of Sarrasin work], in which her unborn son was to be conceived
is described as already decorated with scenes of his exploits. This provides a major ironic reversal of time; it is a visual illustration of the
reflection on paradox that is the theme of the text. Eustache Deschamps's treatise is a denunciation of excessive subtlety and of the
power of logic to lead one astray, to the point of losing one's identity.
Geta's leitmotif when he is dispossessed of his self by the god and is
speaking in another's voice is "Ce suy je qui a moy parole!" (l. 554), or
"Ce suy je qui parole a my" (l. 598) [This is myself speaking to me].
Being is engulfed in the redoubled echo:

> Mais je ne sçay raison ne droit
> Pour quoy uns soit deux orendroit;
> Car c'est chose toute commune:
> Toute chose qui est est une:
> Ne suy pas uns, dont suis je nient.
> Et ceste chose onques n'avient
> Que ce qui est perde son estre.   (Ll. 599–605)

> [But I know neither reason nor right by which *one* should
> henceforth be *two,* for it is a widely shared opinion: every
> thing that is, is one. I am not one, thus I am nothing. And
> it is something that has never yet happened, that something
> that is loses its being.]

What Is Said in the Throat of the Text

Speech is given concrete form as the tongue, the body organ but also the organ of language. It is Jupiter's tongue darting into Alcmena's mouth when he kisses her that betrays his licentiousness:

> Et l'estraint en baisant ses dens,
> Li lance sa langue dedens,
> Cil qui semble a ses baisiers baux
> Qu'il soit uns estrange ribaux.   (Ll. 187–90)

> [And this man, whose audacious kisses make him seem a debauched foreigner, holds her close, and in kissing her he touches her teeth and thrusts his tongue into her mouth.]

The tongue as a body organ reveals the roué in Jupiter, but it is the overly clever speech of the "husband" whom Alcmena thinks she is embracing that reveals him to be inhabited by a god. The scene in fact ends with a sudden shift from the level of *la langue* (the tongue; language) to that of *la parole* (the word; speech):

> Mais bien semble dieu de parole.   (L. 191)

> [But in speech he seems indeed a god.]

The interplay between the two possible syntactical constructions of this line (which might also be translated as "the god of speech dissembles well") creates a *mise en abyme* in which the question of truth and appearance flickers back and forth ad infinitum. Does the speech of the false Amphitryon reveal his true essence as Jupiter? Or does it designate the trickster in him, the god of words? Eustache Deschamps's examination of *la parole* operates to the profit of the evident meaning of things and a direct relationship with things, as illustrated by Birrea in the kitchen:

> Soit logicien qui voulra,
> Car Birrea homs demourra.
> A ceuls plaise leur estudie;
> Ma cuisine a moy, quoy qu'om die,

Me plaist et la gresse du pot;
De logique ne serait sot,
Qui ainsi les gens entortille;
Telle science est trop soutille.   (Ll. 951–58)

[Let anyone who cares to be a logician, for Birrea will remain a man. Let them have their study. My kitchen, whatever people may say, suits me, as does the grease from my
pot. I will not be turned into a dunce by a logic that tangles
people up. That science is too subtle.]

We catch an echo here of the pot grease image in Guillaume de
Machaut. There is also a regression to the primary senses: touch and
taste are more trustworthy than one's eyes or ears. In the incarnation
scenes that use the image of the capture of a unicorn, the creature's
sense of smell (not his eyesight, not his hearing) is what attracts him
to the virgin, much like an odor of sanctity. Eustache Deschamps
shows Geta seeking proof of his own existence in his sense of touch:

Adonc se touche de sa main,
Je ne croiray huy ne demain,
Dist il, que noient devenu
Soit ce qui puet estre tenu.   (Ll. 847–50)

[Then he touched himself with his hand. "I will not believe,
either today or tomorrow," he said, "that what you can hold
can become nothing."]

The tongue leaves off speech here for the sense of taste and the savor of things. Birrea has the last word:

Oez ce que je determine:
Je m'en riray en ma cuisine,
Et Amphitrion voist esbatre
Avec ma dame sanz debatre,
Si com il faisoit par avant;
Et Geta soit homs com devant!   (Ll. 1097–1102)

[Listen to what I've decided: I'm going back to «or: I'm going to laugh about it in» my kitchen, and let Amphitryon go

dally with my lady with no further debate «dalliance, *ébats*; debate, *débats*» as he did before «Birrea does not grasp the fact that the god, not the husband, has just enjoyed Alcmena». And may Geta be a man again, as he was before.]

This return to matter and to material things stands in sharp contrast to the exaltation of logic found in the fourteenth century, for example, in the works of William of Occam. Literature offers an extreme form of this model in a number of tongues cut off—the tongue of Philomena (a character in a passage inserted in the *Ovide moralisé*—perhaps written by Chrétien de Troyes), the tongues of tortured peasants, and the tongues of martyred saints, male and female. How could speech be returned to their throats, that second "lap" or second womb? And what sounds would someone make once his or her tongue was cut out? Basic sounds, the first stammerings of a return to origins, the ABCs, so to speak. This was what happened when Wistace le Moine cut out a servant's tongue:

> Dont commencha a barbeter.
> Dist li quens: "Dyables! C'as tu?"
> Et cil a dit: "Belu, belu,"
> Qui la langue avoit trenchie.
> *(Li Romans de Witasse le Moine, ll. 649–52)*

[He then began to stammer. The count said: "The Devil! What's wrong with you?" And the man who had his tongue cut out answered him, "Baa, baa."]

But by miracle one might also hear clear speech, and the victim's first words might be ones of adoration and jubilation. This is what happened in the case of St. Longinus, whose martyrdom is described in Jacobus de Voragine's *Golden Legend,* in the case of St. Leger, and in the miracle of St. Christina, told by Christine de Pizan as a final counterpoint to the scene of *aombrement* discussed above. On two occasions, succoring angels appear to St. Christina in her dark dungeon, bringing her nourishment and encouragement:

> Et si comme elle estoit la, pensant aux tres grans misteres de Dieu, trois anges vindrent a elle a tout grant lumiere et luy apporterent a

mengier et la reconforterent. . . . Et pource que elle sans cesser
nommoit le nom de Jhesu Crist, il luy fist coupper la langue; mais
mieulx que devant et plus cler parloit adès des choses divines et
beneyssoit Dieu, en le regraciant des benefices que il luy donnoit.

(*Le Livre de la cité des dames*, pt. 3,
chap. 10, pp. 1004, 1008)

[While she was there, contemplating the extraordinary mysteries
of God, three angels came to her in great radiance and brought her
food and comforted her. . . . And because she unceasingly pronounced the name of Jesus Christ, he had her tongue cut out, but
then she spoke even better and more clearly than before, of divine
things and of the one blessed God, thanking Him for the bounties
which He had given her (Richards translation, 236, 239).]

Finally, a severed tongue could produce something other than gur-
glings or miraculous speech, something not to be heard but to be
read like a text. This is what happened to Philomena and her weaving in the *Ovide moralisé*:

Et comance par grant estuide
S'uevre tel come il li sist.

.   .   .   .

Tot ot escrit an la cortine.   (Vol. 2, bk. 6, ll. 3322–23, 3327)

[She reflects no further but immediately sets to work. . . .
She worked it all on the tapestry (Cormier translation,
248–49, 251, ll. 1106–7, 1131).]

There is one oddity that merits a remark: several of these texts
take pains to note at what distance from the root the tongue had
been cut off. Thus in *Philomena*:

La langue li tret de la gole,
S'an tranche pres de la meitié.   (Ll. 3070–71)

[He yanks her tongue from her mouth and cuts off nearly
half (Cormier translation, 238–39, ll. 854–55).]

Christine de Pizan is equally specific:

Et le faulx Julien, qui ceste voix ot ouye, blasma les bourriaulx et
leur dist que ilz n'avoyent pas assez pres couppee la langue de

Christine; si luy couppassent si pres que tant ne peust parler a son Crist. Si luy errachierent hors la langue et luy coupperent jusques au gavion. Et celle cracha le couppon de sa langue au visaige du tirant et luy en creva l'ueil. Et luy dist aussi sainement que oncques mais . . . "Et pource que tu ne cognois ma parolle, c'est bien la raison que ma langue t'ait aveuglé."

(*Le Livre de la cité des dames,* pt. 3, chap. 10, sec. 283, p. 1009)

[The treacherous Julian, who heard this voice, castigated the executioners and said they had not cut Christine's tongue short enough and ordered them to cut it so short that she could not speak to her Christ, whereupon they ripped out her tongue and cut it off at the root. She spat this cut-off piece of her tongue into the tyrant's face, putting out one of his eyes. She then said to him, speaking as clearly as ever . . . "And because you did not heed my words, my tongue has blinded you, with good reason" (Richards translation, 239–40).]

The material, corporeal organ ripped from the body's shadowy interior takes away the light of an eye that truly did not see, for it refused to recognize the Christ, the Incarnation. To blind that eye was to give it access to the truth of its own ignorance. Inversely, but for the identical purpose of demonstrating the power of God, the blood flowing from Christ's wounds gives Longinus back his physical sight, and it provides him with access to a spiritual sight and a life of the spirit. Unsealing someone's eyes snatched him from error.

The tongue as a body organ served as one possible image for a filiation that could be cut at varying distances from the root, as if the tongue, a sharp sword but an organ susceptible to castration, established a relationship with the father rather than the mother. This was a relation to Latin, the language of authority and of the symbolic father, in the case of *Philomena* and, in the case of St. Christina, a relationship to Christ. In moving from the lap or womb to the throat we have moved from the rude to the subtle; from what could neither be cut nor spoken to what could be clearly articulated; from the shadows (*ombre*) to the number (*nombre*) and the name (*nom*).

5 ∎ *Matter for Poets*

Those who merited the title of *poète* in the fourteenth century—
Guillaume de Machaut, Christine de Pizan—reflected on models for
the birth of matter: the model of Christ, first, which was birth by incarnation and by the miracle of love; second, the model of the birth
of the Antichrist, which was a birth without a mother, by cutting, by
incision, by extraction from the womb of a dead mother. In a less
ambitious fashion, they were also interested—as were others—in
ways to renew existent subject matter. Here they explored two routes
simultaneously: the modification of latent schemes and the fitting of
new themes into already constituted molds.

From the Duel to the Triad: Arms, Loves, and Compilations

During the fourteenth century, writers began to translate texts
into French for political and strategic reasons—*pour les armes*—but
poets had long written in French for amorous reasons—*pour les
dames*. Dante recalled in the *Vita nuova* (30.6): "E lo primo che co-
minciò a dire sì come poeta volgare, si mosse però che volle fare intendere le sue parole a donna, a la quale era malagevole d'intendere li
versi latini" [And the first person who began to write as a poet in the

vulgar tongue was moved to do so because he wished to make his words intelligible to a lady who could not easily understand Latin verse (Norton translation, 57)]. *Armes et Amours* was the dual insignia that the fourteenth century chose in a heroic continuation of an attitude more appropriate to the twelfth-century knights of chivalry. Storing up treasures and maintaining past acquisitions provided the leitmotif of the age, the motivation behind the creation of the Court of Love, and the function of that court.

Arma virumque cano, "I sing of arms and the man," Virgil proclaimed in the first lines of the *Aeneid*. Armed combat and love were the two topics still being sung about—usually in combination—in the princely courts of the fourteenth century. Jean de Condé gave the conjunction of the themes a mythic origin. In his *Recors d'armes et d'Amours* he imagines an agreement struck, well before the sieges of Thebes and of Troy, between Mars and Venus:

> Or sont il. ij. mestier ensanle
> Et bien aviennent, ce me sanle.
> Quel sont il? D'armes et d'amours.
> Si doit on pour vaillant tenir
> Qui à droit les voet maintenir,
> Car ensanle sont biel et gent.
>
> (*Dits et contes*, 2:97, ll. 1–2, 4–7)

[There are two trades that go well together, it seems to me. . . . What are they? Arms and love. Anyone who rightly wishes to maintain them should be considered valiant, for together they are beautiful and noble.]

The accord that Jean de Condé presented as a mythic tale is presented with the help of an allegorical figure by his contemporary and fellow countryman Watriquet de Couvin. Narrative and image were favored modes for experimentation with exposition during the fourteenth century. Watriquet tells us that on Ascension Day 1319 he had a vision in which he saw a female monster with two heads but only two feet who spoke to him "à voix de seraine" [in a siren's voice] to declare, "Nous sommes Armes et Amours" [We are arms and loves]. What were these Siamese twin sisters doing? They were guarding an empty seat in Paradise, the seat of Artus de Bretaigne, the king who had united chivalry and courtesy. The dreamer objects that King Arthur died five hundred years after the death of Christ; why, then, is the seat unoccupied? The apparition replies that it is because Arthur is not dead:

> Tant que sire Charles durer
> De Valois au siecle pourra,
> Le bons rois Artus ne morra.
>> (*Li Dis des .IIII. sieges,* in *Dits de Watriquet de Couvin,*
>> ll. 202–4)

[As long as Lord Charles of Valois lives in this world, good King Arthur will not die.]

Charles de Valois, through whom King Arthur lived, according to Watriquet, and who maintained arms and love, was the brother of Philip the Fair (Philippe le Bel) and kin to Gui de Blois, the minstrel's protector. This was the way to pay court to a protector, according to the custom of the time. But Watriquet also admits, obliquely:

> Tiex aime amer qui het combatre,
> Ch'avient en cest monde souvent.   (Ll. 155–56)

[Some love love who hate war; that happens often in the world today.]

Longstanding values were in danger, threatened on all sides, undermined by the behavior of the nobles themselves, and coveted by other levels of society. But although those values might at times be abandoned in practice, they continued to be proclaimed, as authors attached to princely courts knew well. If they chose another subject than *armes et amours,* it was in full awareness of taking a marginal, even transgressive, stance that went against the tastes of their chivalric public. Watriquet de Couvin says as much at the beginning of his *Despit du monde,* a moral poem:

> Dit vous ai d'armes et d'amours,
> Or vous commencerai aillours,
> Mais qu'il ne vous veulle desplaire.
>> (*Dis de Watriquet de Couvin,* 155, ll. 1–3)

[I have told you of arms and loves. Now I am going to begin on another subject *«aillours* marks the departure», but may it not displease you.]

A minstrel was not in a court to preach. Others took care of that. But without denying the traditional chivalric and amorous subject matter, the fourteenth-century authors attempted to help it to evolve and to change the equilibrium of the whole by adding a third term to the couple, *armes* and *amours*. This was the subtle game that Guillaume de Machaut played. In the *Voir-Dit,* Guillaume proposed one formula, "Armes, dames, et conscience" (letter 10 of the lover, p. 68) [arms, ladies, and conscience]; in *Le Remede de fortune,* he offered another, "Armes, amours, autre art ou lettre" (*Oeuvres,* vol. 2, l. 40) [arms, love, other art or letter (Wimsatt and Kibler edition, 170)].

What is important from a structural viewpoint is the breakup of the binary scheme and the appearance of a third term or series of third terms that cannot be subsumed into one of the other two terms. What is significant from a semantic viewpoint is the introduction of the book, literature, and reflexivity into the canonical pair. That the book might replace arms and love was a notion that operated according to the theory of the ages of man, a device that served as a mold for the thought of the time. An individual's life was seen in terms of that theory; it provided a grid for reading literary works. The contrast between the first and the second parts of *Le Roman de la Rose* was based on it. When the century was thought of as a whole, it bore the characteristics of old age: one of these was avarice (in literary terms, a penchant for storing up treasures), but love of books— a substitute for the love of women, which advancing age made less likely—was another. Youth was the time for arms (in war or in the hunt) and for love—for the pleasures of the *veneur* and of Venus, linked in Guillaume de Digulleville's etymology of the goddess's name. To old age—the real kind or that brought on by the death of a loved one—belonged the book and writing, and, for some, it led to a certain form of wisdom. Jean de Courcy (b. 1360) explicitly thought of his life in just such terms. He wrote in the prologue to his compilation of ancient history, which he titled *La Bouquechardière* in reference to his own name (he was the lord of Bourg-Achard in Normandy): "Moy, Jehan de Courcy, chevalier normant, plain de jours et vuydie de jeunesse . . . ay commencé compilacions . . . par ce que mon pouoir n'a pas esté si fort que j'aye peu mon corps exposer ou fait de la guerre" (MS, fol. 3, Fonds français 329, Bibliothèque nationale, Paris) [I, Jean de Courcy, Norman knight, burdened with days and emptied of my youth, . . . have begun compilations . . . because I have not strength enough to expose my body to warfare]. He identifies himself in a later work of some forty thousand lines, *Le Chemin de vaillance,* in these terms:

> Moy Jehan de Courcy, qui traittié
> Ay en viel aage ce traittié
>
> .   .   .   .
>
> En mon an soixante sixieme.
>> (MS 14 E. II, fol. 294r, col. b, British Museum, London
>> [French text])
>
> [I, Jean de Courcy, who have composed this treatise in my old age . . . at the age of sixty-six years.]

The career of Antoine de La Sale (b. ca. 1386) followed a similar pattern: a man of arms until he turned fifty, he then set about compiling works to which he, like Jean de Courcy, gave titles—*La Salade, La Sale*—that bore his name. He wrote these works for the edification of the sons of his protectors, *La Salade* for Jean de Calabre, the son of René d'Anjou, *La Sale* for the three sons of Louis de Luxembourg. The literary production of Petrarch and Charles d'Orléans was organized according to a similar division between books of their youth and books of their old age. Charles V turned this idea into policy by replacing the power of arms with that of language and books.

This shift produced a discernible renewal in literature. Certain places, seasons, and objects replaced others as topical motifs, or, more subtly, they framed the older motifs, throwing them slightly off kilter. The barren plain replaced the orchard of love; autumn replaced springtime; the conjugal bed, the setting for a serious debate between spouses in Antoine de La Sale's *Le Reconfort de Madame de Fresne,* and even the bed of the dying man dictating his last will and testa-

ment pushed the love bed into the shadows, where it had to wait several centuries before it found its place in the *alcôve*.

Fourteenth-century literature made positive use of the second degree,
the "once removed"—a second reading that it nonetheless considered
a limitation—by exploring the possibilities of a late or indirect entry
into a text. In this manner, Guillaume de Machaut's *Le Jugement dou
roy de Navarre* opens in autumn, "au departir dou bel esté" (l. 1) [at
the passing of a beautiful summer (Palmer translation, 3)]. The poet,
gripped by melancholy, retreats to his chambers. He meditates on
change, always for the worse. There is no more harmony in family relations:

> Car je ne voy pere,
> Fil, ne fille, ne suer ne frere,
> Mere, marrastre, ne cousine,
> Tante, oncle, voisin, ne voisine,
> Mari, mouillier, amy, n'amie
> Que li uns l'autre ne cunchie.　　(*Oeuvres,* vol. 1, ll. 53–58)

> [For I see no father, son, no daughter, no sister, no brother;
> mother, relative, or cousin, aunt, uncle, neighbor, husband,
> wife, lover or beloved, such that the one doesn't deceive the
> other (Palmer translation, 5).]

Avarice reigned. Men's folly found an echo in the folly of the
world, a sure sign of God's wrath:

> Car il sambloit que decliner
> Voisist li mondes et finer.　　　　　　　　　(Ll. 305–6)

> [For it seemed that the world wanted to come to an end.]

This gloomy picture was not an isolated instance. It puts into perspective the casuistic amatory debates that took place only when
springtime returned, when the plague subsided and its parade of
woes was less threatening (thus giving the topos of renewal its
strongest meaning). This scenario for delayed debate reflects a debate
introduced more directly in *Le Jugement dou roy de Behaingne.* That
text opens, in canonical fashion, with the line, "Au temps pascour

que toute riens s'esgaie" (l. 1) [In the Easter season, when every creature takes heart (Palmer translation, 3)], that was itself an echo of the
lyrical tradition—more precisely, in my opinion, of the first lines of
a composition by Bernard de Ventadour: "Lo gens tems de pascor /
ab la frescha verdor" (*Chansons d'amour,* no. 17, ll. 1–2). Who suffered
more, a lady whose lover had died or a lover whose lady was unfaith-
ful? In other words, who suffered more in love, the man or the
woman? *Le Jugement dou roy de Navarre* responded to the *Jugement
dou roy de Behaingne* in an autotextuality that explicates what it
meant to rethink an old debate in 1349.

In *Le Livre du dit de Poissy,* Christine de Pizan shifted the balance
of the traditional question. For her it became, Who is the more unhappy, the lady whose lover has been taken prisoner by the Turks or
the squire whose lady has rejected him? Historical reference, which
serves to anchor the question, had penetrated the debate. Christine's
book opens with a springtime scene in which green grass, the song of
the birds, and a soft morning all go to create a harmonious scene.
This is a setting not for a love scene, however, but for a mother's desire to visit her daughter, who is a nun. The springtime topos deviates
from its usual function in a subtle (and deliberate) shift from one sort
of love to another, a move that serves to throw the debate off center
and to relativize its meaning.

In *La Fonteinne amoureuse,* Guillaume de Machaut effects another
type of displacement. He begins his *dit* with a night scene (rather
than a *matinet*), but it is a night that brings no dreams. The poet, half
asleep (in *la dorveille*), hears the lament of a lover on the other side of
the wall, and he transcribes what he hears. The dream that we expect
is set awry. It takes place the next day, not by night but by day, not in
the enclosed space of the bedchamber but in a park, induced not by
a psychological state of melancholy but by the physiological fatigue
of a sleepless night.

This was playing with the topos. To avoid the boredom of repetition, fourteenth-century writing raised a desire for an expected subject matter and, by that very token, renewed it. From the viewpoint
of form, this was done by modifying the narrative or topical econ-

omy of expected places and schemata. From the ideological viewpoint, it was done by giving those elements a new equilibrium (or by setting them off balance) by use of a framing thought introducing a new context. This was a way of assembling materials in order to defer expectations and play with desire; it was writing in the proper sense of the term. It relied on the melancholy reverie of delayed departures and on an exploration—joyous or sad—of the question of point of view.

Something New under the Bright Sun?

The fourteenth century renewed subject matter by displacement. It also regenerated it by substitution. At the end of the twelfth century, Jean Bodel, in his *Chanson des Saisnes,* gave narratives three possible fields, catagorizing them according to their degrees of truth and usefulness:

> Li conte de Bretaigne si sont vain et plaisant,
> Et cil de Ronme sage et de sens aprendant,
> Cil de France sont voir chascun jour aparant.   (Ll. 9–11)

> [The tales of Brittany are frivolous and pleasant, and those
> of Rome wise and instructive. Those of France are true, as
> is evident every day.]

Jean Le Fèvre inventoried topics differently in 1376 at the beginning of his *Respit de la Mort,* which took as its point of departure the thought, shared by all of Jean's contemporaries, that there was nothing new under the sun: "Soubz le soleil n'est rien nouvel" (l. 11). This later time saw disenchantment, a crisis in subject matter, pessimism. Jean Le Fèvre continues, listing negatively (an approach by rejection that is itself symptomatic) all the topics that he did not intend to treat:

> Pour acquerir gloire,
> je ne voeil pas traitier d'amours
> ne d'armez, ne faire clamours
> de Fortune ne de sa roe
>
> .   .   .   .

Soubz le soleil n'est rien nouvel,
ne de Renart ne de Louvel.   (Ll. 4–7, 11–13)

[In order to acquire glory, I do not intend to treat of love or
of arms, nor compose laments about Fortune and her
wheel. . . . There is nothing new under the sun, neither
about Renard nor about the Wolf.]

Jean Le Fèvre rejects lyrical subject matter (*amours*), epic subject
matter (*armes*), and even didactic subjects, whether allegorical (Fortune) or presented as a fable. Only one subject was worth writing
about: death.

J'ay asséz aillieurs a entendre
a ce qui revertist en cendre.   (Ll. 9–10)

[I have enough to keep me busy elsewhere with what returns to ashes.]

Aillieurs, the adverb "elsewhere," defines the position of all these
writers in relation to their subject matter: they stand to one side of it,
behind it, or a bit away from it. Their position defines their gaze and
their structural place. We have seen this with Watriquet de Couvin;
it occurs in Jean Le Fèvre; with Christine de Pizan it becomes the
very definition of the woman, the widow, and the writer. Theirs was
no longer a poetics of joy and of belonging but one of sadness. Jean
Le Fèvre states, "mon enque destempay de larmes" (l. 54) [I diluted
my ink with my tears]. Charles d'Orléans states that when he writes
he dips his pen into "l'eaue d'Espoir" [the water of Hope], which has
become inky black under the effect of melancholy: "D'elle trempe
mon ancre d'estudie" (*Poésies,* vol. 2, rondeau 325, p. 478, ll. 9–13).

Since the motive force of love no longer functioned, "la matere
fault" [matter was lacking], as Guillaume de Machaut noted in the
Voir-Dit. In this text the lover-poet complains to his lady after his
first crisis of doubt as to her fidelity: "Mais puis que matere me fault,
il me convient laissier oeuvre" (letter 30 of the lover, p. 238) [But
since I lack matter, I would be better off abandoning the work]. At
the moment of his second fit of doubt he raises the stakes: "Et certes
je ne fis rien en vostre livre puis Pasques, et pour ceste cause; ne ne

pense a faire puis que matere me faut" (letter 42 of the lover, p. 342) [And admittedly I have not worked on your book since Easter, and for that reason; and I do not think I shall work at it, since I lack matter].

Matter without love, without *fin amour,* became a martyrdom. The rhyme *matyre/martyre* appears in Guillaume de Machaut. We read in *La Fonteinne amoureuse,* in the *confort* that the lady brings her lover in a dream:

> Mais qui autre mercy desire
> Et qui dit qu'il pleure et soupire,
> Dont il le couvient a martyre
> Vivre et manoir,
> Il a tort et assés s'empire.
> Venus scet bien ceste matyre.
>
> (*Oeuvres,* vol. 3, ll. 2335–40)

[But someone who desires greater favor, saying that he weeps and sighs, and this forces him to live and remain in suffering, does wrong and harms his cause. Venus knows this line well (Palmer translation, 213).]

Courtly love was the only imaginable kind. The rhyme soon became obsessive, martyrdom having subsumed matter by its sound. In *La Prison amoureuse,* by Jean Froissart, the lady complains in a virelay of her situation,

> dont j'ai bien matire
> De douleur et de martire.   (Ll. 3212–14)

[from which I have much matter for pain and martyrdom.]

If the lady could no longer be the object of hopeful love and if the beloved lady's demeanor forbade dreams, another lady took her place, the Virgin. As Guillaume de Machaut states in *Le Lay de la fonteinne:*

> S'en vueil une autre acointier
> Qui joie pleniere
> M'otriera de ligier.   (*Poésies lyriques,* lai 16, ll. 9–11)

[Then will I want to bind myself to another, who will lightly grant me total joy.]

The Holy Virgin Brings A New Sound

Marian poetry had brought a strong current of renewal to amourous subject matter since the thirteenth century. In *Les Miracles de Nostre Dame,* Gautier de Coinci taught that the old love poetry must be abandoned to permit a regenerated poetry to flow forth:

> Chant Robins des robardeles,
>> Chant li sos des sotes,
> Mais tu, clers qui chantez d'eles,
>> Certes tu rasotes!
> Laissons ces viés pastoreles,
>> Ces vielles riotes;
> Si chantons chançons noveles,
>> Biaux dis, beles notes
>>> De la fleur
>> Dont sanz sejor
> Chantent angeles nuit et jor.   (3:293, ll. 39–49)

[Let Robin sing "robinades" for coquettish women, let fools sing foolish songs for fools, but you, clerk, who sing of women, truly you have lost your head! Let us leave off these old pastorales, these old debates; let us sing new songs, fine poems, beautiful songs on the flower of whom the angels sing ceaselessly day and night.]

The new, sweet subject matter was the unique mother, the Virgin. Here too, rhyme—*mère/matière*—is indicative of this new poetry and one of its preferred technical devices. Gautier de Coinci illustrates this renewal in another form of displacement—*contrafactum*—when he grafts a secular refrain into his song:

> Chascun an fas de la virge sacree
> Un son nouvel, dont tout l'an me solas.
> Dire puet bien qui a s'amor bien bee:
>> "Vous ne sentez mie
>> Les dous maus d'amer
>> Aussi com je fas."   (3:297, ll. 5–10)

> [Every year, I make a new song on the holy Virgin that consoles me all year long. It can speak for someone who desires her love: "You do not feel the sweet pangs of love as I do."]

Just as the angel's message to Mary renewed humankind, the Virgin renewed poetry. *Ave* made up for *Eva:* "Ce nous renouvelle," Guillaume de Machaut exclaims in *Le Lay de Nostre Dame* (*Poésies lyriques,* lay 15, l. 44).

But there were other sorts of regeneration and other substitutes for the lady. Cities and towns inspired a powerful love in the fourteenth century, one that gave the poets something else to write about.

The Thought of the City

The city merited being sung of and written about because the city was a woman and, as such, was the very stuff of poetry. In its guise as a female, the city was caught in a tension between praise and blame; it was the place of all temptations and all excesses but also of all pleasures and rewards. It was both Jerusalem and Babylon, Eve and Mary. As Petrarch wrote to Francesco Nelli (Petrarca, *Sine nomine,* letter 10), Avignon was Babylon, a great harlot, the scarlet woman of the Apocalypse (Rev. 17.4–5).

But the city, like the woman, was also a text, and a poetic text. This was true, first, because they inspired the same poetic genre. In twelfth-century lyric poetry, the farewell to the woman had given rise to the genre of the aubade; the farewell to the city created a new genre of leave taking, first in the form created in Arras during the thirteenth century and later, during the fourteenth century, in forms with a variety of objects. Eustache Deschamps wrote adieus to Paris, Reims, Troyes, and Brussells. The sensuality of an entire epoch can be read in such inventories. Farewells invoke the pleasures of love, of the table, of language, and of speech. Eustache Deschamps has one "fillette" (a young prostitute) boast of her "bon cul de Paris" (*Oeuvres complètes,* 4:8, no. 554, l. 15) [nice Parisian derriere]. Selling her charms she calls out in the refrain, "Sui je, sui je, sui je belle?" [Am I

Missal, Paris, c. 1425–35.

Book of Hours, Poitiers (?), c. 1425–35.

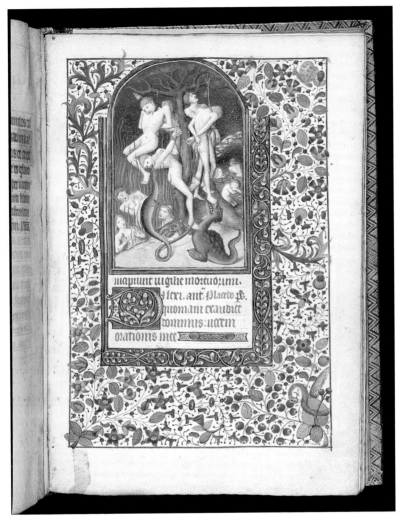

Book of Hours, Savoy, c. 1460–70.

Book of Hours, Paris and Loire region (?), c. 1470.

Book of Hours, Paris, c. 1475–80.

Book of Hours, Loire region (Tours?), c. 1500.

Book of Hours, Paris (?), late fifteenth century.

Book of Hours, Tours (?), c. 1535.

beautiful?]; François Villon praises Parisian speech in *Le Testament* with the refrain, "Il n'est bon bec que de Paris" (l. 1522) [There is no tongue like one from Paris (Bonner translation, 103)]. There was poetry in the cries of the city's street vendors. Eustache Deschamps made an erotic pun on the *connins* that says he left behind regretfully: "connins, plouviers et capons et fesans" (4:6, no. 552, l. 9) [rabbits, plovers, and capons, and pheasant]. "Adieu connins, perdriz que je reclaims" (5:52, no. 871, l. 7) [Farewell rabbits, partridge that I crave].

This was an old pun. But the metaphoric network changed between the hunt for *connins* of the *Roman de la Rose* (vol. 2, l. 15110) and the *amoureuse cuisine* of the fourteenth and fifteenth centuries. Charles d'Orléans used "dedans l'amoureuse cuisine" as the refrain of one of his rondeaus (vol. 2, rondeau 283). We have moved from the chivalric space of the hunt to "bourgeois" images of the kitchen, from an open space to a closed one, from a tension springing from desire to the temptations of pleasure.

Like a woman's name, the very name of a city could become a phonic mold for the renewal of poetry. There is a fine example of this in a piece attributed to Eustache Deschamps, *Paris ethimologié* (10:83–85, no. 75). Each stanza begins with the repetition of one letter in the name of the city: "Par plusieurs poins peut Paris precellence" [In several points Paris can be awarded prime excellence]. The name Paris appears in this poem written out, letter by letter, in all directions, horizontally and vertically, in a multidirectional anagram. The letters of its name are enclosed, as if shut up in a jewel box, in such words as *paradis, saphir, séraphin*. This was "rhétorique ravie" [delighted rhetoric] and "subtilité semée" [broadcast subtlety]. Eustache—if indeed he was the author, or his imitator, if not—sowed widely the name of Paris, and a poetic style sprang from that seed. It was a style founded on number, on abundance: *mille* was one of the key rhymes, along with *subtille* and the adjective *ville* (lowly, base) for the noun *ville*. The city was inebriating, and giddiness is embedded in the poem's enumerative style and reeling inventories. Words are repeated, as are phonemes, forming series that give an image of the tensions that were an integral part of city life. The initial *p* in Paris gave *Paris sans per* (peerless Paris), an alliteration originally applied to Paris, the Trojan prince and mythical hero, but that serves here for *perdriz* (partridge) and *petits pastez* (little pastries) as well.

Finally, the city was a text because it was a memory—by name, first, which fitted into the important question of origins, filiations, and invented fathers and genealogies (Paris for Paris, Remus for Reims); second, thanks to its monuments and the traces of the past they bore, to which writers were becoming more sensitive (we need only think of Jean Froissart); and third, by its history. The theme of *ubi sunt* functioned as well for cities as for women: Where now are Troy, Babylon, Niniveh, and Rome? Eustache Deschamps wondered. Their stones and their splendor may have disappeared, but they remained present in memory and in writings. For a man, the city was a descendance created by his subtlety and his art, which might be furthered by his natural progeny. Christine de Pizan had the dying Epaminondas declare: "Je ne meure pas sans hoir, car je vous laisse deux filles que je vous ay engendrees; et ce vouloit il dire deux nobles cités qu'il avoit acquises car il n'avoit nuls hoirs de son corps. Si entendoit que par ces deux cités conquestees demorast la memoire de lui si comme fait par les enfans des peres" (*Le Livre du corps de policie,* 40) [I do not die without heirs, for I leave you these two daughters I have begotten (he meant these two cities, because he had no heirs of his body). He understood that he would live in memory because of these two cities he had conquered, just as children remember their fathers (Forhan translation, 24)].

In much the same manner, in Eustache Deschamps reflection on the city was accompanied by reflection on *la langue* (in all the senses of the term) and on writing. The envoi to *Paris ethimologié* concludes:

> Vous qui voiés Paris *auctorizé*
> En cinq letres contraintes a loy dure.
> (*Oeuvres complètes,* 10:85, no. 75, ll. 56–57)

> [You who see Paris clothed in authority by five letters constrained by a harsh law.]

The city had become an author and an authority.

The fourteenth century had an urban model of the text, no longer solely in its subject matter and its thematic material but also in its very organization. The composition of the *dit*, in fact, was no longer linear—based on a narrative line or an unfolding aventure—but fragmented. The text became a labyrinth (for Petrarch, Avignon was a gilded labyrinth). It was a palace in which one lost (and found) one's way and one that concealed both treasures and monsters—Dedalus and the Minotaur.

We have moved from the forest, the antithesis of the book and book culture (think of Pierre de Celle and St. Bernard warning monks to flee from the midst of Babylon if they wanted to save their souls) to the exaltation of the book in a city setting. We have moved from the *liber* to the *livre* by means of the *libation:* the city was the place of the tavern, and Petrarch read *avinio* (given to wine) in the name Avignon. But even Petrarch, who developed a taste for one form of the solitary life, recognized the importance of the city and its knowledge:

> Throughout my life, it has rarely happened, if I was in good health, that I let a day of leisure go by without reading, writing, meditating on letters, listening to reading or interrogating those who are now silent, and I have not only sought knowledge from men but also in cities in order to return more learned and better: the first was Montpellier, because during the years of my childhood I lived close to that place, soon it was Bologna, then Toulouse and Paris, Padua and Naples.
>
> (Petrarca, *De ignorantia,* quoted in French in Michel, *Pétrarque et la pensée latine,* 161)

A new subject matter began to appear during the fifteenth century. It began with Alain Chartier, a figure who served as the starting point for a new canon in a number of domains. The new mother and the new matter was France. But that brings us to the threshold of another epoch.

The One Who First Found ("Cil qui premier trouva")

Writers of the fourteenth century offered a third response to the crisis in subject matter. Matter was no longer to be engendered, either on the incarnation model or the incision model. (As an example of the latter: Bacchus—Dionysus—the twice-born god, was ripped by Zeus from the womb of his mother Semele, the daughter of Cadmus and Harmony, who had been killed by Zeus's thunderbolts. Zeus then sewed the child into his thigh to be reborn later in a second and paternal birth.) Writers turned from renewing subject matter to inventing it.

In his definitive *Europäische Literatur und lateinisches Mittelalter* (*European Literature and the Latin Middle Ages*), Ernst Robert Curtius speaks of "'Who discovered it?' . . . a question which was dear to the hearts of the Greeks and which may well be called characteristic of their thinking" (Trask translation, 548). This theme reappeared massively in the French Middle Ages. We can see it in several forms. It entered into the praise of famous persons, lists of whom the age, following Boccaccio, was fond of compiling and in which "cil qui premier trouva" [the one who first found] was a prime element. It was an important moment in the topos of praise of the arts. Every treatise that reviewed the liberal arts began with their origin and cited the name of their "inventors." Finally, it appeared, as if by chance (a sign of its vitality and its strength), in a variety of narrative, lyrical, and moralistic texts. Thus Alain Chartier, in *Le Debat des deux fortunés d'Amours,* speaks through one of the two knights to credit love as the great inventor:

> Amours trouva premier haulx instrumens,
> Chançons, dances, festes, esbatemens,
> Chappeaulx de fleurs, jolis habillemens,
> Joustes, essais, bouhours, tournoiemens.
>
> (*Poetical Works,* ll. 651–55)

[It was Love who first invented musical instruments, songs, dances, feasts, amusements, flowered wreaths, handsome clothing, jousts, assaults, rejoicings, tournaments.]

This statement is followed by a long list of all the joyous inventions of Love. Charles d'Orléans praised the "inventor" of writing in a ballade in which he takes consolation in writing to his lady when he can no longer speak to her:

> Loué soit cellui qui trouva
> Premier la maniere d'escrire.
> (Poésies, vol. 1, ballade 21, ll. 1–2)

[Praised be he who first discovered how to write.]

The prior in Guillaume Alexis's *Passetemps des deux Alecis freres* pays hommage to the "inventor" of music:

> Qui premier trouva la pratique
> De la science de musique
> Pour accorder si proprement,
> Avoit moult bel entendement.
> (Oeuvres poétiques, 2:8, ll. 17–20)

[The person who first discovered the practice of the science of music in order to make such perfect harmonies had very good judgment.]

What did this infatuation with origins mean? Complex notions enter into the concept of invention. In the first place, except for one occurrence in the Cambridge Psalter in the sense of "expedient" or "ruse" and its use in the expression *invencion Sainte Croix* (the discovery of the True Cross), the word *invention* is not found in Old French. It appears in its modern sense in the fifteenth century. The first mention noted in Walther von Wartburg's etymological dictionary dates from 1431. The word can be found in this meaning, however, in Christine de Pizan's *L'Avision Christine,* a work written in 1405. The speaker is Dame Opinion, whom Christine presents as the daughter of Ignorance, fathered by Desire for Knowledge. From Dame Opinion "vindrent . . . les premieres invencions des fais" (*La-vision-Christine,* 134, l. 11) [the first invention of human deeds comes from you (McLeod translation, 86)]; it was she who gave Alexander "l'invencion d'emprendre les fortes et fieres batailles" (135, l. 29) [«the inspiration» to wage great and fierce warfare (McLeod translation, 80)]; it was thanks to her that Christine herself got the idea—though at the time she had little idea of the power of invention—of writing *Le Livre de la mutacion de fortune:* "Combien que par moy te venist l'invencion" (131, l. 21) [You came to the discovery because of me (McLeod translation, 77)]. Philosophy's handmaiden Opinion put *invention* within the reach of human understanding in all domains of activity. Christine insists on this point: "Dame, puisqu'il est ainsi que de vous vient la premiere invencion des oeuvres humaines bonnes ou mauvaises, rudes ou soubtilles" (143, ll. 17–19) [Lady, since the first invention of human deeds—good or bad, crude or subtle—comes from you (McLeod translation, 86)].

It was Dame Opinion who made the first men seek out the properties of herbs and plants: "Et tres ces premiers aages furent aucuns soubtilz hommes auxquelz tant fis encerchier qu'ilz trouverent philosophie. Et par consequent toutes les sciences et ars par moy furent premierement investiguees, et la voye trouvee d'y attaindre; ne nom de philosophe oncques trouvé n'eust esté se je ne fusse" (112, ll. 11–16) [From the earliest times, there were a few clever men whom I incited to such inquiry that they discovered philosophy; all the arts and sciences were thus investigated—and the way to reach them was found—because of me. If I had not existed, Philosophy would never have been discovered (McLeod translation, 61)].

The word *adinvention* is attested, in the modern sense of "invention," around 1310. Gilles Li Muisis used it frequently, always in a pejorative context, either in the semantic network of an imitation or caricature of the creative power of God (the theme of the monkey) or in the broader sphere of novelty, which he disapproved of. The appearance of this word and lexically related words is highly significant. By the fourteenth and fifteenth centuries, the question of invention and inventors had found a prominent place on the literary agenda.

How had the notion of *invenire* been translated before that time, given that the other verbs that express the same idea in Latin—*reperire*, for example—had disappeared in Romance? All the lexicons and all the translations of medieval texts that I have consulted concur: the Latin notion was expressed exclusively by the verb *trover,* to find. This one-to-one equivalence highlights one of the prime questions that the concept of invention posed in the Middle Ages—the status of invention in relation to creation and, as a corollary, the status of invention in relation to God. Only God could create. He was the *droit createur,* as Jean Le Fèvre recalled with some anxiety concerning possible counterfeits:

> Que vault enquerir par grans cures
> de toutez choses lez naturez,
> a ceulz qui partinaulz deviennent
> et contre verité soustiennent
> leur fausseté et leur malice?
> Le faiseur de tout artifice
> et le droit createur oblient.
>
> (*Le Respit de la Mort,* ll. 2521–27)

[What need have those who persist, obstinate in error and sustaining their falsity and their malice against the truth, to seek with such great care the natures of all things? They forget the one who made all the arts and who is the true creator.]

What did the inventor do, then? He found. The distinction between creation and invention (*troveure, trovement*) is confirmed by all the texts. The precision of the vocabularies in these instances is heavy with theological import. Brunetto Latini proclaims at the start of his *Livre dou tresor,* "Le mal fut trovés par le diauble non pas criés," and he adds, "et por ce est il noiens, car ce ki est sans Dieu est noient" (bk. 1, chap. 11, p. 26) [Evil was found by the devil and not created; that is why it is pure nothingness, for that which is without God is naught].

Invention would always retain some trace of its sulfurous, diabolic genealogy; it was, by definition, vain. The first attested meaning of *invention*—"expedient," or "ruse"—is proof of this. The compound form *controver,* a possible substitute for *trover,* was even more clearly marked as diabolical. Like *adinvention* in relation to *invention,* the meaning of *controver* in relation to *trover* became fixed, as the centuries passed, to reflect values of mendacity and trickery. By its morphological formation, *controver* clearly indicates the mimesis inherent in all human creation. Human endeavors were always inscribed *contre* —that is, in reference to—a model, the ultimate model being divine creation. It would be interesting to study the evolution of a similar pair of words, *faire* (to do) and *contrefaire* (to counterfeit) and to examine the replacement of *contrefaire* by *imiter* in the late Middle Ages.

The appearance of the word *invention* and a concentration on the theme of the inventor signaled a partial desacralization and secularization of thought. It made possible consideration of the problem of human creation (or what passed for it), in particular, the problem of aesthetic creation. The terms *oeuvre* and *adinvention* were frequently coupled in translations of the Bible. Could man, like God (or like the Devil), be *opifex* or *artifex*? Was there anything left to "find," or did one have to invent? And if so, just what was "inventing"? The word *novus* shifted from having negative to positive connotations during the thirteenth century. In the fourteenth century, the word *innover* (to innovate) entered the language.

For the clerks of the Middle Ages, there was a historical answer to this problem. They were less prone to philosophical interrogation and more apt simply to ask who was the inventor of some phenomenon or how one invention had followed another. Origin was seen as an explanatory principle; the problem was to see what had come out of it. Reflection on invention focused less on asking what was upstream than on exploring what had gone on downstream. This was historical thought, inasmuch as history is succession.

Thought about invention also concerned names. Invention was connected with the presence of a name that had made things happen, with the rise of an individual, a heroic founder, the point of departure of a lineage. There was increasing interest, during the fourteenth and fifteenth centuries, in the notion of the individual. The inventor gave his name to his invention. He showed proof of authority by imposing a name, but he also kept to his own place in the order of creation. Like Adam in the Book of Genesis, the inventor created nothing; he named things. Was the domain of the *logos* thus the place reserved to man? This would make invention mean causing something new to appear in a way that did not compete with divine creation. Invention was not so much the manipulation of matter as the manipulation of forms, which explains the importance accorded to metamorphoses in this literature.

The *Ovide moralisé* appeared in the fourteenth century. Invention appealed less to reason than to *mètis,* the clever, practical, even mechanical sort of intelligence (a notion that brings us back to the first meaning of *invention*) that this age saw as embodied in the concept of subtlety. Invention had an obvious function. If it was an answer to the crisis of subject matter that haunted the poets, this was not in the humble form of the gleaner (an image also present in the same authors) but in the prideful and chivalric model of the family tree. Drawing up a catalogue of inventors was a way to inscribe one's own name—at times explicitly, more often incidentally—in a prestigious lineage. The new pride of the clerk thus found expression without disrespect to the notion of lack of polish, the topos of modesty currently in vogue. By setting up an intellectual genealogy (and, by implication, placing himself at the end point of the lineage he enumerated), the clerk-writer gave himself *lettres de noblesse* (in all senses of the term). Establishing a catalogue was one way to reflect on one's own practice and to create an archaeology for it. This was the role this line of thought and writing played and the ends it served.

Benoît de Sainte-Maure touched on this theme in the twelfth century. In his description of Argus constructing a ship he states:

> Co vuelent dire li plusor,
> Mais jo nel truis mie en l'autor,
> Que ço fu la premiere nef
> Ou onques ot sigle ne tref,
> Ne que primes corut par mer.
> Cil qu'i osa premiers entrer,
> Co fu Jason, ço est cuidé,
> Mais n'en truis mie autorité.
>
> (*Le Roman de Troie,* vol. 1, ll. 913–20)

[Several gave it to be understood, but I do not find it in the source, that this was the first ship that bore sails and masts and the first that cleaved the seas. Jason was the first person who dared enter into the ship, as was imagined, but I do not find any authentic attestation of it.]

This reflection on the invention of navigation (first ship builder, first navigator), which, as he takes care to note, Benoît failed to find in his source, is significant when we know that elsewhere he compares his own writing to navigation. Toward the middle of this work he declares:

> Mout par ai ancore a sigler,
> Quar ancor sui en haute mer.   (Vol. 2, ll. 14943–44)

[I still have much navigating to do, for I am still on the high seas.]

Benoît pursues the metaphor, with a play on words between *ancre* (anchor) and *encre* (ink), asking God to grant him the privilege of completing the voyage and casting anchor in a safe habor: "Qu'a dreit port puisse ancre geter!" This concern for inventors marks Benoît as a writer prone to reflection. His transfer of ancient myth to a vernacular narrative was just as much an innovation, in its raw materials and its object, as Jason's voyage in the ship Argus had built.

Two centuries later, Guillaume de Machaut gave a more fully elaborated form of the same topos in a reflection on a particular variety of "translation," metamorphosis. The passage occurs during the first dream of the *Voir-Dit,* when the King Who Does Not Lie (le roi qui ne ment), a "king" in a game, reproaches the poet, suggesting that the latter would not be so upset by the change of color of his lady's robe from blue to green (a sign of disloyalty) if he thought of the extraordinary metamorphoses described by Ovid. Furthermore, the King Who Does Not Lie states:

> On voit et scet tout en appert
> Que moult furent sage et appert
> Cilz qui les sciences trouverent
> Et aus peuples les lois donnerent.   (Ll. 5362–65)

[One sees and knows clearly that those who found the sciences and gave the peoples laws were very wise and very intelligent.]

The king goes on to list some of these: there was Jabel, the inventor of sheep herding, Jubal (as the manuscripts states, not Tubal, as in Paulin Paris's edition of this work), who "trouva l'art de musique" (l. 5380) [found the art of music]; there was Noëma (Naamah), who invented the art of weaving; Chus (Shem, the second son of Noah), "qui trouva la science / Que l'en appelle nigromance" (ll. 5394–95) [who invented the science called necromancy]; Phoroneus, who "donna les lois / Tout premierement aux Grijois" (ll. 5402–3) [first gave the Greeks laws]. At the bottom of the list came the seven sages of Rome and Pythagoras, the inventor of mathematics. The king comes to the conclusion that all these sages could not advise the poet in love, whose only option was resignation. The king expresses this thought emblematically in a proverb, "Laisses Amour convenir" (l. 5457) [Let love do what it will]. Love and Wisdom were two separate domains. By this means Guillaume de Machaut signals the tension between the love poem (courtly lyricism) and the clerk's poem (learned didacticism) that makes his poem come to life. The King Who Does Not Lie subtly reminds the poet of his place among the inventors,

Jubal trouva l'art de musique,
Tubcaÿn trouva la fabrique,
Mais Jubal au son des martiaus
Fist tons et sons, et chans nouviaus
Et notés, et les ordenances
De musique et les concordances,

adding,

Et s'aucuns y ont amendé,
Je ne leur ay pas commandé.   (*Voir-Dit,* ll. 5380–87)

[Jubal found the art of music; Tubal-Cain found how to make instruments, but Jubal, to the sound of the hammers, composed tones, sounds, and songs, new and noted, and

the organization of music and the harmonies; and if some
have bettered that, I have not told them to do so.]

Who but the poet, as Paulin Paris suggested, could be depicted
under this mask of *aucuns*? The enumeration set up a genealogy, and
the title for inclusion in it was intelligence. The word *titre* (title) appears, what is more, in the following passage, where it rhymes (in
rime riche) with *tistre* (weaving):

> Et Noëma trouva le tistre
> Et le filer, quar a son tiltre
> On fait linges et draperies
> Et les belles toiles delies.   (Ll. 5388–91)

[Noëma found the art of weaving and spinning, for it is
thanks to her that linens and draperies and beautiful, fine
cloths are made.]

This genealogy was no longer based on children begotten in nature's
way, a model that Guillaume recalls, speaking of the birth of Jabel
and Jubal:

> Cilz .II. furent frere
> Issus d'un pere et d'une mere.   (Ll. 5372–73)

[Those two were brothers, born of one father and one
mother.]

It was a genealogy based on a birth without a mother, a birth of the
spirit, like that of Minerva issuing from the head of Jupiter. The
clerks, whose filiation was intellectual, were one illustration of this
birth. A new nobility came to be created, a new class whose aim was
no longer to live for love and sing of love but to write about wisdom
and the arts. This is what we read between the lines when the King
Who Does Not Lie indirectly reproaches the poet for not speaking
enough about wise men:

> De dire leur sens et leur euvres
> —Dont il m'est vis que petit euvres,
> Quant ainsi ies envelopés
> D'amourettes et attrapés—

Certes longue chose seroit
A dire qui la te diroit.   (Ll. 5436–41)

[To speak of their intelligence and their works—to which it
seems to me you pay too little attention, you who are so
taken and tangled up in your love affairs—certainly would
take a long time should anyone want to explain it to you.]

The personal promotion of the clerk and the institutional promotion of wisdom are two aspects of the role of the topos that were su-
perbly illustrated in the work of Jacques Legrand. That Augustinian
monk put himself on the list of inventors not, like Guillaume de
Machaut, for his role in perfecting music but rather for making im-
provements in the alphabet. In the portion of his *Archiloge Sophie*
that speaks of the liberal arts, Legrand first recalls that the first language, Hebrew, had been "found" by Abraham, then goes on to consider Greek and Latin letters and their inventors. He concludes:
"Mais tu pourroies demander se les lectres latines sont souffisans a es-
cripre tout ce que nous pouons prononcier. Et dient les communs
gramairiens que elles sont souffisantes sans autres lectres trouver"
(*Archiloge Sophie,* 65, ll. 6–9) [But you might ask whether Latin letters are sufficient to write everything that we might pronounce. Most
grammarians say that they are sufficient, hence there is no need to
find other letters].

Jacques Legrand was not of that opinion (nor was Eustache Deschamps). He thought that the ambiguity in the written forms of *v*
and *j*—letters that could be interpreted either as consonants or as
vowels—should be eliminated. He added, insisting on the conven-
tionality of the alphabet: "Car il n'est point de doubte que les lectres
furent figurees de propre voulenté, et pour tant raison ne contredit
point a ce faire" (65, ll. 20–21) [For there is no doubt that the letters
were imagined by deliberate decision, and, by that token, reason does
not contradict the notion of imagining others].

Jacques Legrand depicts himself as an inventor. He tells us why he
is interested in reflection on the arts, their birth, and their historical
filiation. For him, the question is timely because it enables him to

understand the reasons for the decline, or at least the unsteadiness, of the kingdom: "Et de fait les Grecs et les Rommains sont tousjours decheus depuis l'eure qu'ilz delaissierent les estudes, comme il appert au jour dui" (43, ll. 18–20) [And in fact the Greeks and the Romans always fell into decadence the moment they left off study, as it is clear today].

The lessons of universal history were applied to the present day. It was a good thing to go beyond the current error that declared knights to be ashamed of being thought clerks: "Et de fait chevalerie est a ceste erreur venue que c'est honte a un chevalier d'estre clerc reputé" (43, ll. 13–15). Eustache Deschamps concurred ("Car chevaliers ont honte d'estre clercs" [*Oeuvres complètes,* 3:187–89, no. 401, refrain), and he drew the same conclusion: what was needed was a return to a union of *fortitudo* and *sapientia,* a return to the inventors. As early as the thirteenth century, *L'Image du monde* by Maître Gossouin had proposed that objective. Criticizing the clerics of Paris who yearned for the name of *maistre* but "qui pou sevent de raison et de bien" [who know little of reason or good], Gossouin offered the model of the inventors of the arts: "Car cil s'ordenerent autrement aus arz, qui premierement les trouverent" [For those who first found them devoted themselves to the arts in a different manner]. He concluded: "Tout en tele maniere ordenerent les .VII. arz cil qui premierement les controuverent" (75) [Those who together first discovered the seven arts ordered them in that manner].

Among the various realizations of the topos of invention, the scenario of the invention of writing took on special importance during the fourteenth and the fifteenth centuries. Its frequency corroborates the notion that the clerks were deeply aware of the change represented by the shift from oral to written vernacular literature. To speak of "invention" was to speak of the *inventeur*—the inventor—which meant that a cultural hero stood at the inception of the technical achievement of writing.

We need to distinguish between three types of mythical personages who had some connection with the mystery of letters. The first is the figure of the magician or the divine, referred to here emblematically under the name of Orpheus, given in some Greek texts as the inventor of the alphabet. The second figure is that of the scribe, the intermediary, the secretary. This is Thoth, the Egyptian god. The third figure is that of the founding hero, the founder of a city and inventor of the alphabet. It is this last configuration that will occupy us in particular. Two heroes competed for the spotlight in the literature of the late Middle Ages—a man, Cadmus, and a woman, Carmentis, respectively, the inventors of the Greek alphabet and the Latin alphabet. Fourteenth- and fifteenth-century authors used these heroic figures in three ways. First, they inscribed them within a reflection on the *translatio studii,* the transfer of knowledge from the East to the West. In this interpretation, Cadmus and Carmentis were associated with Io (Isis), with whom they formed a triptych depicting the invention of Egyptian, Greek, and Latin letters. The model for that presentation and its founding text came from Isidore of Seville: "Aegyptiorum litteras Isis regina, Inachis filia, de Graecia veniens in Aegyptum, repperit et Aegyptiis tradidit. . . . Cadmus Agenoris filius Graecas litteras a Phoenice in Graeciam decem et septem primus attulit. . . . Latinas litteras Carmentis nympha prima Italis tradidit" (*Etymologiarum,* bk. 1, chap. 3, secs. 5 and 6; chap. 4, sec. 1) [Queen Isis, the daughter of Inachus, coming from Greece into Egypt, found Egyptian letters and gave them to the Egyptians. . . . Cadmus, the son of Agenor, first brought from Phoenicia to Greece seventeen Greek letters. . . . The nymph Carmentis first gave Latin letters to the Italians].

Jacques Legrand repeated this presentation in his description of the *.VII. ars liberaulx,* and it became the standard treatment in all treatises on the arts: "Les grecques lectres trouverent jadis et premierement les Phenis, gens ainsi nomméz comme tesmoigne Lucan le poete. Mais Cadmus filz de Agenor, fut cellui le quel premierement presenta .XVII. lectres grecques" (*Archiloge Sophie,* 61, ll. 20–23) [The Phoenicians—people so named, Lucan the poet tells us—were the first, long ago, who found the Greek letters. But Cadmus, the son of Agenor, was the first to present the seventeen Greek letters]. "Et de fait nous lisons que la royne nommee Ysis, la quelle fut fille de Inaché, fut celle qui premierement apporta les lectres aux Egipciens. Et dient aucuns qu'elle les aporta de Grece en Egipte, et les autres dient que elle les trouva a sa venue de Grece en Egipte et les donna aux Egipciens" (63, ll. 1–5) [And in fact we read that the queen named Isis, who was the daughter of Inachus, was the first who brought letters to the Egyptians. And certain people say that she brought them from Greece to Egypt, and others that she found them coming from Greece to Egypt and gave them to the Egyptians]. "Aprés tu dois savoir que jadis une deesse nommee Carmentis fut celle qui premierement donna aux Ytaliens les lectres latines" (64, ll. 12–13) [You must then know that long ago a goddess named Carmentis was the first who gave the Italians Latin letters].

The second model used Carmentis, either alone or in association with Io, with the polemic aim of defending women and demonstrating their creative capacities. Here the basic text was Boccaccio's *De mulieribus claris,* written in 1361 and first translated into French in 1401 under the title, *Des Femmes nobles et renommées.* Another French translation, offered in 1493 to Queen Anne and published by Antoine Vérard, was entitled *Des Nobles et cleres femmes.* As early as 1370–71, however, Carmentis was mentioned in French by Jean Le Fèvre in his *Livre de Leesce,* a refutation of the *Lamentations* of Matheolus, which Jean Le Fèvre translated. He first lists a number of women who were outstanding for their courage, then women who shone in the domains of the arts and sciences:

> Car Carmentis trouva l'usage
> Des lettres de nos escriptures,
> Toutes les vint et cinc figures
> Dont on puet en latin escripre,
> En françois, en tables, en cire,
> En papier ou en parchemin;
> Carmentis trouva le chemin:

A chascune mist propre nom;
De sens doit avoir grant renom. (Ll. 3623–31)

[For Carmentis found the use of the letters of our writings,
the twenty-five signs thanks to which one can write in
Latin, in French, on tablets, on wax, on paper, or on parch-
ment. Carmentis opened the way; she gave each one its
name; she merits great renown for her intelligence.]

There are three things to note in this presentation. Jean Le Fèvre
displays a high degree of sensitivity to the various material supports
for modes of writing (*en tables, en cire, en papier ou en parchemin*) and
to different realizations (*en latin, en françois*). Clearly, there was a profound connection between French and Latin for all learned people of
the late Middle Ages. There was no need to reinvent the alphabet; a
few adjustments in Latin letters would suffice for the notation of
French. Jean Le Fèvre's precision was shared by other authors who
took special pains to specify the number of letters invented by each
hero. We can see the same care in *Le Respit de la mort*. In a passage on
study that follows arguments against marriage, Jean Le Fèvre states:

Les uns aprendent a escrire
de greffes en tables de cire.
Les autrez sievent la coustume
de fourmer lettres a la plume,
et paingnent par dessus les piaux
et des moutons et des viaux,
et a coulourer se doctrinent;
il flourettent, il enluminent.
Les autrez apliquent leurs cures
a plus soubtillez escriptures,
a gramaire puis a logique,
et a parler par rectorique. (Ll. 2411–22)

[Some learn to write with a stylus on a waxed tablet. Others
follow the custom of forming letters with a pen, and they
paint on the skins of sheep and calf and learn to color; they
paint flowers, make illuminations. Others occupy them-

selves with more subtle writings, with grammar, then with
logic, and with speaking according to rhetoric.]

This shift from a reflection on generation to a meditation on writing
is not anodyne. The passage is in the lineage of *Le Roman de la Rose*
of Jean de Meun, and it echoes his use of the figure of Cadmus in the
context of possible metaphors for generation.

Jean Le Fèvre also uses the image of the path or road, a spatial image taken from the intellectual lineage of the *translatio studii*. For all
these authors, study is a road (after all, one of Christine de Pizan's
works is entitled *Le Chemin de long estude*). One of its models was the
human life span, or the "pilgrimage of human life," as in the title
of one of Guillaume de Digulleville's works. Jean Le Fèvre gave this
advice:

> Mais qui ne congnoist dont il vient,
> la ou il est ne qu'il devient,
> soit riche, povre ou mendiant,
> il n'est pas vrai estudiant.
> Pour ce devons ymaginer
> la ou nous convient cheminer,
> et adviser en nous meismez
> ou nous sommez, dont nous venismez,
> entre nous de l'umain lignage
> qui alons en pelerinage.   (*Le Respit de la Mort*, ll. 2573–82)

> [But he who knows not from whence he comes, who knows
> not where he is nor where he is going, whether he is rich,
> poor, or a beggar, does not study the truth. For that very
> reason, we ought to think where we should be going and
> consider within ourselves where we are, from whence we
> come, we, the lineage of humans who go in pilgrimage.]

Finally, we need to note the new importance that Jean Le Fèvre
gives to the very act of naming. To "invent" was also to name: giving
a name to the letters, giving one's name to an invention. Hence, reflection on invention goes hand in hand with etymology. The example of Phoroneus, "cil qui premierement / Controuva plait et jugement" (*Le Respit de la Mort*, ll. 3843–44) [the one who first found law

trials and judgments], as it is developed in the *Ovide moralisé*, bears witness to this:

> De son non sont plait surnomez:
> En latin sont "fora" nomez.   (Ll. 3847–48)

> [With his name were trials named: in Latin they are called "fora" «law courts; the forum standing for judiciary eloquence».]

In the series of texts written in honor of women and in defense of the female sex, Carmentis (also known as Nicostrata) always occupies a place of choice. In chapter 3 of book I of the *Archiloge Sophie,* Jacques Legrand uses Carmentis in both this role and a historical role:

> Pluseurs par sapience femmes sont renommees
> Comme les dix prophetes Sebilles surnommees;
> Et Carmentis, Ysis, Minerve et Libye,
> Semiramis, Juno, Opis et Marpesye.   (34, ll. 5–8)

> [Several women are renowned for their wisdom, like the ten prophetesses called the Sibyls; and Carmentis, Isis, Minerva, Libya, Semiramis, Juno, Ops, and Marpesye.]

Carmentis has an important place in Christine de Pizan's *Le Livre de la cité des dames,* where she marks a shift of topic and a new step in the argument. Not only are women capable of adding luster to the arts that have already been created and even of excelling in them; they are also capable of inventing arts. Christine cites Carmentis as the earliest example of this:

> Et premierement te diray de la noble Nycostrate,
> que ceulx d'Italie appellerent Carmentis.
>   (Pt. I, chap. 33, p. 735)

> [First I will tell you of the noble Niscotrata whom the Italians call Carmentis (Richards translation, 71).]

Nicostrata's genealogy is interesting. Christine says:

> Ceste dame fu fille du roy d'Archade nommé Pallent. Elle estoit de merveilleux engin et douee de Dieu d'especiaulx dons de savoir.

Grant clergesce estoit es lettres grecques et tant ot bel et saige langaige et venerable faconde que les pouettes de lors, qui d'elle escriprent, faignirent en leurs dittiez qu'elle estoit amee du dieu Mercurius; et un filz qu'elle avoit eu de son mary qui en son temps fu de moult grant sçavoir, disdrent qu'elle l'avoit eu d'icelluy dieu.
(Ibid.)

[This lady was the daughter of a king of Arcadia, named Pallas. She had a marvelous mind, endowed by God with special gifts of knowledge: she was a great scholar in Greek literature and had such fair and wise speech and venerable eloquence that the contemporary poets who wrote about her imagined she was beloved of the god Mercury. They claimed that a son whom she had with her husband, and who was in his time most learned, was in fact the offspring of this god (Richards translation, 71).]

Carmentis was connected with Mercury (Hermes)—that is, with the god of *mètis,* the clever, practical, technological sort of intelligence. According to tradition, as Christine prudently says, she was a friend of the god's; in the tradition followed by Antoine Dufour in *Les Vies des femmes célèbres,* she was his daughter: "Les poètes faignent que Mercure fut son père" (45). Both authors emphasize (Christine with discretion, Antoine Dufour more blatantly) the possible illegitimacy of her son, a point important for my argument. "Pour ce que l'on ne treuve point que jamois fut mariée, tant pour sauver son honneur que pour veoir estranges pays, fist charger force navires et emmena avecques elle son petit filz Palentin et arriva à Hostie sur le Tybre" (*Les Vies des femmes célèbres,* 45) [Because it has not been found that she had ever been married, as much to save her honor as to see new lands, she had many ships loaded, brought with her her young son Palentin, and arrived at Ostia on the Tiber].

In the mythical birth of writing as in the geneaology of natural lineages, there is an obscure point, a void at the point of origin, to which the act of foundation proper is linked. It is clear that Christine identifies with Carmentis. Both women had a strong connection with Italy. Carmentis arrived there from Greece ("ariva sur le fleuve du Tybre" [*Le Livre de la cité des dames,* pt.1, chap. 33, p. 785]) [she arrived at the river Tiber]); Christine had left Italian lands for France, continuing the *translatio studii* that Carmentis had begun. Carmentis was a builder—"La, celle dame, avec son filz et ceulx qui suivie l'avoyent, fonda un chastel" (ibid.) [There, this lady and her son and all those who had followed her built a fortress (Richards translation, 71)]—as was Christine, who used the stories of Carmentis and other illustrious women as building blocks for her City of Ladies. Finally, Carmentis was a prophetess (Christine was the daughter of an astrologer) and gave her name to song: "De ceste dame Carmentis furent nommez dittiez *carmen* en latin" (738) [Poems were named *carmen* in Latin, after this lady, Carmentis (Richards translation, 72)].

Christine de Pizan never abandoned lyric poetry, which remained one of the prime aspects of her creative achievements. We read in the French adaptation of Giovanni Balbi's *Catholicon:*[1] "Carmentis, propre nom de fenme et vaut tant comme deesse de dictié" [Carmentis, female proper noun and signifies goddess of poetry]. The following entry reads: "carmino, nas . . . ou carminor . . . naris . . . faire dictié ou charmer ou charpir lainne" [to make poetic compositions, make charms, or card wool].

"Deesse de dictié" was just what Christine de Pizan wanted to be. As Guillebert de Metz recalled in his *Description de la ville de Paris* in 1407, Christine "dictoit toutes manieres de doctrines et divers traitiés en latin et en françois" [composed all sorts of teachings and various treatises in Latin and in French]. Eustache Deschamps summed her up as "Muse eloquent entre les .IX., Christine" (*Oeuvres complètes,* 6:251, no. 1242, l. 1) [Muse most eloquent among the nine, Christine].

After her appearance in the works of Christine de Pizan, Carmentis was cited consistently by authors who took the side of women and wrote in their honor. She is mentioned by Martin Le Franc in *Le Champion des dames:* "de dame Carmente, laquelle trouva la lettre latine" (MS, fol. iiiv, Fonds français 12476, Bibliothèque nationale, Paris) [of lady Carmentis, who found Latin letters]. She is also men-

1. Mario Roques, ed., *Recueil général des lexiques français du Moyen Age (XIIᵉ–XVᵉ siècles),* vol. 1, *Lexiques alphabétiques,* pt. 2 (Paris: Champion, 1938).

tioned by Symphorien Champier in *La Nef des dames vertueuses* (1503); by Antoine Dufour in *Les Vies des femmes célèbres* (1504); in *La Chasse d'Amours,* attributed to Octovien de Saint-Gelais and published by Antoine Vérard in 1509; and in *El Triunfo de las donas* by Juan Rodríguez del Padrón. Not only is she mentioned, but Carmentis enables us to grasp these authors' attitudes toward knowledge, learning, and writing. One illustration of this occurs in a context other than the *querelle des femmes* (debate about women). In his *Doctrinal du temps présent,* Pierre Michault borrows a passage from the *Sophilogium,* the first version of Jacques Legrand's *Archiloge Sophie.* Virtue guides the author on a visit to the *ancienne escole* (ancient school): "Tu voiz aussi entre les femmes icy paintes, Ysis, qui trouva les lectres des Egipciens; Nicostrates bailla les lectres et orthographie aux Ytaliens; Noctia, soeur de Tubalcayn, trouva les ars mecaniques; les douze Sibilles en maintes prophecies ont descript l'advenement de Dieu" (sec. 34, ll. 9–16) [You see also among the women who are painted here Isis, who found the letters of the Egyptians; Nicostrata gave the letters and spelling to the Italians; Noctia «Naamah», the sister of Tubal-Cain, invented the mechanical arts; the twelve Sibyls, in many prophecies, described the coming of God].

A third model in such speculation regarding the invention of writing divided the actions of Cadmus and Carmentis into the three functions described by Georges Dumézil: the magical and juridical function, the warrior function, and the nurturing function. The stories connected with these two heroic figures clearly display, in terms of the social reality of the Middle Ages, characteristics of the three functions of cleric, knight, and peasant. Three gods took an active part in the destiny of Cadmus: Ares, the god of war, whose creature, the serpent guarding the god's fountain, is killed by Cadmus; Athena, who advises the hero to sow the serpent's teeth; and Aphrodite, whose daughter Harmony (fathered by Ares) he marries. Thus Cadmus is a warrior (he fights the dragon), a farmer, though of a rather special sort (he sows the dragon's teeth), and, as the founder of Thebes, whose king he becomes, a hero of the first, magical and juridical, function. As Georges Dumézil brilliantly demonstrated in his

Apollon sonore, commenting on a text by Plutarch, Carmentis is a heroine of the third, nurturing function: she presides over childbirth. By her powers of prophecy and by her role in furthering civilization, she is also a heroine of the first function. Her second name, Nicostrata, which combines words meaning "army" and "victory," shows a connection with the second function. One can categorize authors and periods during the Middle Ages by their emphasis on one or another of these functions.

Arnoul d'Orléans wrote of Cadmus in his *Allegoriae super Ovidii Metamorphosin* in a passage that persistently connects the warrior model to the clerical model:

> Revêtu d'une peau de lion, c'est-à-dire de fougue, tenant deux javelots, c'est-à-dire muni de faconde et de sagesse, Cadmus, décidé à venger par la discussion, lança contre le serpent un rocher, c'est-à-dire des arguments dépourvus d'efficacité, sans pouvoir nuire au serpent, c'est-à-dire à l'astuce des gens du pays. Mais il les transperça enfin d'un javelot, c'est-à-dire de sentences plus acérées et plus subtiles. Il sema ensuite les dents du serpent, c'est-à-dire inventa les lettres grecques. De là vient que l'on dit: Grecorum primus vestigat gramata Cadmus.
>
> (*Allegoriae,* 3:1; in French translation by
> Demats, in *Fabula,* 192)

> [Dressed in a lionskin (that is, in ardor), holding two javelins (that is, armed with speaking ability and wisdom), Cadmus, intent on taking his revenge by discussion, threw a rock at the dragon (that is, inefficacious arguments) without being able to harm the dragon (that is, the wiliness of the people of that land). But he finally pierced them with a javelin (that is, with sharper and more subtle phrases). He then sowed the dragon's teeth (that is, he invented Greek letters). This is why it is said: Cadmus was the first to trace Greek letters.]

We might note in passing the use of the verb *vestigare* (to follow the trace or track of; to seek; to discover)—also used when Cadmus, seeking his sister Europa, followed the tracks of a cow—rather than *invenire.*

When Jean de Meun speaks of Cadmus (*Le Roman de la Rose,* vol. 3, ll. 19706–22), he places major emphasis on the hero of the third function, the seed sower, the founder of a lineage, the indefatigable plowman. The hero appears in a message (a hymn to generation) brought by Genius, in a passage that Félix Lecoy, the editor of the text, summarizes as follows: "Malheur à ceux à qui Nature a donné stylets et tablettes, marteaux et enclumes, socs aigusés et jachères fertiles ne demandant qu'à être labourées, et qui refusent d'écrire, laissent leurs enclumes se couvrir de rouille et leurs champs retourner en friches" (xxi, summarizing ll. 19513–52) [Woe to those to whom Nature gave styluses and writing tablets, hammers and anvils, sharp plowshares and fertile lands that only needed to be plowed, and who refuse to write, let their anvils become covered with rust and their fields go fallow]. Genius continues, pointing to Cadmus as an example:

> Mout fist Cadmus bone semance
> qui som peuple ainsinc li avance.
> Se vos ausinc bien conmanciez,
> vos lignages mout avanciez. (Vol. 3, ll. 19719–22)

> [Cadmus sowed right well, who thus increased his people. If you too begin well you will increase your lineages.]

Christine de Pizan made subtle choices of emphasis between Cadmus and Carmentis according to the public she was addressing and the argument she was pursuing. In *L'Epistre Othea,* the aim of which is the training of the knight, Cadmus alone appears, and in this context he illustrates the need to combine the clerical virtues and chivalry. Christine concludes her gloss on this example: "Si veult dire Othea que le bon chevalier doit amer et honnourer les clercs letrez, qui sont fondez en sciences" (chap. 28, p. 196) [Othea wants to make it clear that the good knight must love and honor lettered clerics who are well instructed in learned disciplines].

Cadmus also appears in *Le Chemin de long estude* when the Sibyl is telling Christine the history of the fountain of wisdom:

> Jadis Cadmus a moult grant paine
> Un grant serpent sus la fontaine

Dompta, qui avoit pluseurs testes
Et toutes dorees les crestes;
Et c'est le serpent qui destourbe
Moult a aler en celle tourbe.   (Ll. 1075–80)

[Long ago Cadmus, after great effort, vanquished a great
serpent by the fountain who had several heads with golden
crests; it is this serpent who makes it extremely difficult to
join those who gather there.]

To end the list, Cadmus is mentioned in *Le Livre de la cité des
dames,* but only in his role as the founder of Thebes: "et aussi comment Cadmus fonda Thebes la cité par l'admonnestement des dieux"
(pt. 1, chap. 4, p. 631) [and also how Cadmus founded the city of
Thebes with the admonition of the gods (Richards translation, 11)].
Reason predicts to Christine that the city she was going to build
would be more solid than Cadmus's city.

The fact that these writers reflect on inventors, Cadmus and Carmentis in particular, shows that a new conception of the poet was
coming to light at the end of the Middle Ages. Just as the invention
was linked to the name of its inventor, the work came to be tied to
the artist, whose portrait began to be individualized. As Ernest Kris
and Otto Kurz state in *Legend, Myth, and Magic in the Image of the
Artist:*

> Whether or not an artist's name is recorded depends, not upon the
> greatness and perfection of his artistic achievement—even if this
> were objectively ascertainable—but upon the significance attached
> to the work of art . . . Very generally speaking, one can say that
> the urge to name the creator of a work of art indicates that the
> work of art no longer serves exclusively a religious, ritual, or, in a
> wide sense, magic function, that it no longer serves a single pur-
> pose, but that its valuation has at least to some extent become in-
> dependent of such connections. In other words, the perception of
> art as art, as an independent area of creative achievement—a per-
> ception caricatured in the extreme as "art for art's sake"—declares
> itself in the articulation of the growing wish to attach the name of
> a master to his work.   (3–4)

Writers' reflection on Cadmus and Carmentis bears witness to that evolution. It marked a stage in the constitution of the figure of the poet as creator. It also signaled a meditation on progress, since the alphabet was always given as something perfectible. (The insistence on the number of letters invented by the various heroes is pertinent here.) This is why Cadmus and Carmentis were still very much present in literature during the Renaissance: the invention of printing gave them renewed relevance. At the beginning of his *Champ Fleury ou l'Art et science de la proportion des lettres,* Geofroy Tory muses about the invention of the letters and traces the history of the alphabet: "L'invention des lettres a esté diverse, selon diverses opinions" (fol. 5) [As to the invention of letters, there are different opinions (Ives translation, 13)]. He calls on Cadmus and "Nicostrata qui fut autrement nommee Carmentis" (fol. 5v) [Nicostrata, who was also called Carmentis (Ives translation, 14)]. We also find the invention of letters in the emblem "Prefiguration de l'Imprimerie Lyonnoise" at the head of Barthélemy Aneau's *L'Imagination poëtique.*

The contrast between Cadmus and Carmentis is also evidence of an inquiry into the very act of creation, no longer conceived of simply as fiction but now also as foundation. Two models, one masculine, one feminine, stood opposed to one another. The model of Cadmus was agrarian and germinative; it had to do with sowing seeds and with writing as tracing a furrow. The model of Carmentis relied on the voice, which called things into being; it evoked construction, architecture, and art. Was inventing—writing—sowing seeds? Was it construction?

We can begin to understand why there was always a deep complicity in the history of literature between reflection on poetry and meditation on the alphabet.

Leafing through the Book of Memory

Montaigne, in his essay on liars ("Des Menteurs"), states: "Le magasin de la memoire est volontiers plus fourny de matiere que n'est celuy de l'invention" (*Essais,* bk. 1, chap. 9) [The magazine of the memory is generally better furnished with matter than that of the invention (Zeitlin translation, 1:25)]. Memory's storehouse was very much connected with the question of invention. Memory had long been compared to a box: in his *Didascalicon,* Hugh of St. Victor called it an *arcula,* a little chest (bk. 3, chap, 11, "De Memoria"; Taylor translation, 94). Memory—a coffer, an armoire, or a jewelbox— became a book in the fourteenth and fifteenth centuries. In the miniature accompanying the section devoted to Flowering Memory (Flourie memore) in *Les Douze Dames de Rhétorique,* a late fifteenth-century treatise on poetics, Memory is shown seated, with her eyes lowered, writing in a book. A small coffer is open at her feet, and a phylactery winding out of it says, on the lefthand part of the scroll, *nova,* and, to the right, *vetera.* Grave Meaning (Gravité de Sens), another "lady of rhetoric" in the same work (in another manuscript she is called Vielle Acquisition—Old Acquisition), is pictured with a verse legend that reads:

> J'ay un panier porté dès mon enfance
> Que j'ay remply de matères diverses
>
> . . . .
>
> De long pener et invenible cure
> J'ay estoré l'escrin de ma memoire.
>
> (Les Douze Dames, no. 4)

> [I have carried a basket since I was a child, which I have filled with various things. . . . By long travail and incessant care, I have filled the coffer of my memory.]

Thus memory was a coffer that one filled, accumulating treasures, or that one pilfered from. Olivier de La Marche opens his *Mémoires* with this advice: "Et tiercement, se vous trouvez que Dieu ait permis à la fortune que toutes emprinses ne soient pas venues à souhait et selon le desir des haulx entrepreneurs, que ces coups de foüetz et divines batures fierent et hurtent à la porte de vostre pensée pour ouvrir le guichet de sage memoire, affin que vous doubtiez et creniez les persecutions du ciel" (1:13–14) [And third, if you find that God has permitted fortune «to arrange things so» that all enterprises have not ended up according to the desires and the wishes of their initiators, may those whiplashes and those divine blows knock and pound at the door of your thought to open the little door of wise memory so that you will dread and fear heaven's persecutions].

A similar image can be found in François Villon when he speaks in *Le Lais* of *l'entr'oubli* (half-forgetfulness):

> Lors je sentis dame Memoire,
> Reprendre et mectre en son aulmoire
> Ses especes colaterales. (Octave 36, ll. 284–86)

[Then I saw Dame Memory take up and place in shelves her dependent species (Bonner translation, 17).]

Reason summons Jean Meschinot, the author of *Les Lunettes des princes,* in these terms: "Mon enffant, esveille tes espriz et ouvre l'escrin et coffret de ta memoire, pour loger ce beau don et present que liberalement et de bon vueil te donne" (34, ll. 91–93) [My child, awaken your mind and open the treasure box and coffer of your memory to put in this fine gift and present that I give you, generously and with good will]. Reason's gifts were the book of conscience and eyeglasses that enabled their wearer to read it.

Charles d'Orléans shuts up the heart of his lady "ou coffre de [sa] souvenance" (ballade 32) [in the coffer of his memory]. In another ballade, the same coffer contains a mirror that he has bought from Love:

> Mettre le vueil et enfermer
> Ou coffre de ma souvenance,
> Pour plus seurement le garder.
> (*Poésies*, vol. 1, ballade 35, ll. 24–26)

[I want to put it and lock it up in the coffer of my memory to keep it more securely.]

Time is secreted away. There are a number of scenarios that touch on this theme. In one, a book is found in an armoire or in a monastery library and is translated. A dual process of opening up is involved here, part spatial (opening the armoire), part symbolic (opening up the language—Latin—which was closed to the laity, as was the clerical library). The *Cligès* of Chrétien de Troyes begins in the following manner:

> Ceste estoire trovons escrite,
> Que conter vos vuel et retraire,
> En un des livres de l'aumaire
> Mon seignor saint Pere a Biauvez;
> De la fu li contes estrez. (Ll. 18–22)

[The story I wish to recount to you, we find written down in one of the books of the library of Saint Peter's Cathedral in Beauvais; the tale was taken from there (Staines translation, 87).]

Le Bestiaire, a thirteenth-century work by one Gervaise, begins similarly, with the author stating that he had translated a book found in an armoire at Barbery, a Cistercian abbey near Bayeux.

Similarly, the *Roman de Troie en prose* states in its epilogue: "[Si vos ai] ore menee a fin la veraie estoire de Troie, selon ce que ele fu trovee escritte el l'almaire de Saint Pol de Corynte en grezois langage, et dou grezois fu mise en latin, et ge l'ai translatee en françois" (MS, Fonds français 1627, Bibliothèque nationale, Paris) [I have now finished the true history of Troy, as I found it written in Greek in St. Paul's library at Corinth, and from the Greek it was put into Latin, and I translated it into French]. The epilogue to *Queste del Saint Graal* states: "Et quant Boorz ot contees les aventures del Seint Graal telles come il les avoit veues, si furent mises en escrit et gardees en l'almiere de Salebieres, dont Mestre Gautier Map les trest a fere son livre del Seint Graal por l'amor del roi Henri son seignor, qui fist l'estoire translater de latin en françois" (279–80) [When Bors had related to them the adventures of the Holy Grail as witnessed by himself, they were written down and the record kept in the library at Salisbury, whence Master Walter Map extracted them in order to make his book of the Holy Grail for love of his lord King Henry, who had the story translated from Latin into French (Matarasso translation, 204)].

The scenario of invention by a happy discovery and a *translatio* can also be found in the *Cymbalum mundi* of Bonaventure Des Périers and other works. The *Cymbalum* begins: "Il y a huyct ans ou environ, cher amy, que je te promis de te rendre en langaige françoys le petit traicté que je te monstray, intitulé *Cymbalum mundi,* contenant quatre dialogues poetiques, lequel j'avoys trouvé en une vieille librairie d'ung monastere" (1) [About eight years ago, dear friend, I promised you that I would render into French for you the little treatise that I showed you entitled *Cymbalum mundi,* containing four poetic dialogues, that I had found in an old bookcase in a monastery].

Another way of presenting a work was as a book found in a tomb. This is the opening of the French translation of the *De vetula,* a work attributed to Ovid: "Ci commence Ovide de *La Vieille,* translaté de latin en françois par Maistre Jehan Lefevre, procureur en Parlement. Et fut trouvé ce livre en un petit cofret d'ivoire en la sepulture du dit Ovide IIII^c ans apres sa mort, tout frais et entier" (Jean Le Fèvre, *La Vieille ou les dernières amours d'Ovide,* 1) [Here begins *The Old Woman* by Ovid, a text translated from Latin into French by Master Jean Le Fèvre, a lawyer in the Parlement. And this book was found in a small ivory coffer in the tomb of the said Ovid four hundred years after his death, in good condition and complete].

Finally, there was the scenario of the book found, completely worked out, in the "treasury" of the author's own memory and transcribed by him. Michault Taillevent's *Le Songe de la toison d'or* ends:

> Mychault aprés son premier somme
> Trouva ce dit en son tresor
> Et pour ce prie qu'on le nomme
> Le songe de la thoison d'or.
>
> (Ll. 739–42, in *Le Passe Temps,* 83)

> [Michault, after his first sleep, found this poem in his treasury, and for that reason he asks that it be called "The Dream of the Golden Fleece."]

Jean Meschinot's *Les Lunettes des princes* used the same device of conscience offered by reason, as did this prayer of Guillaume Crétin to the great masters of the poetic art:

Abbé d'Auton, et maistre Jehan Le Maire,
Qui en nostre art estes des plus expers,
Ouvrez l'archet de vostre riche aumaire,
Et composez quelque plainte sommaire
En regrettant l'amy qu'ores je pers.
(*Plainte sur le trespas [de] Guillaume de Byssipat,* in *Oeuvres
poétiques,* 174, II. 541–45)

[Abbot «Jean» Auton and Master Jean Lemaire «de Belges»,
you who are the most expert in our art, open the treasury of
your rich libraries and compose some pithy lament to
mourn the friend I have now lost.]

Among the Tombs, among the Pages

The cemetery, the memory, and the book were parallel spaces.
The cemetery, as a way to mark space and the passage of time and as
a new way to mark culture, is everywhere in the literature of the fourteenth and the fifteenth centuries. A stroll amid the tombs became a
lyrical and narrative commonplace that circumscribed genres and set
the pace for melancholy imagery. Obviously, the cemetery had existed as a setting for fiction even in previous literature. There are famous cemetery scenes like the one in *Le Chevalier de la charrete* of
Chrétien de Troyes. The differences are fundamental, though. In the
twelfth and thirteenth centuries, the cemetery was a setting for an adventure or an exploit. The knight showed his valor by combating a
demon, as in *Amadas et Ydoine,* a text of the late twelfth century, or
in *L'Atre périlleux,* a mid-thirteenth century work that bears a telling
title, given that *âtre* or *aître,* derived from the Latin *atrium,* designated the ground next to the church that served as a cemetery. It was
a place for trials of strength, as with Lancelot's feat in *Le Chevalier de
la charrete,* or for receiving a revelation of one's destiny. In that same
work, the tombs, turned toward the future, await their dead:

Et s'avoit letres sor chascune
qui les nons de ces devisoient
qui dedanz les tonbes girroient.   (Ll. 1860–62)

[On each «tomb» were carved letters forming the names
of those who would be buried there (Staines translation,
193).]

Lancelot, who has not revealed his name at this point in the tale,
raises the stone covering one of these tombs, an exploit that normally
required seven men (l. 1897). The stone bears the message:

> Cil qui levera
> cele lanme seus par son cors
> gitera ces et celes fors
> qui sont an la terre an prison.   (Ll. 1900–1903)

[The man who lifts this stone by himself shall be the libera-
tor of all men and women imprisoned in the land (Staines
translation, 193).]

The cemetery was prophetic; it was to be read in the perspective of
resurrection, when tombs would open and deliver up their dead.

Many other cemeteries encountered in the literature of the fourteenth and fifteenth centuries serve a different end. Turned toward
the past, their stones and their monuments preserve names from
oblivion. This was how the cemetery wove its relationship with
memory—something that seems obvious to us today, but it bears
noting that it had a historical origin. Similarly, we can see the word
souvenir and the allegorical figure that stands for memory change in
value as they were used from one century to another. As a force of the
virtual and a figure connected in its essence with hope, *souvenir*
slipped into the sphere of the past and of melancholy. Two nearly
contemporary examples express this notion, albeit differently. For
Charles d'Orléans, *souvenir* still retained its traditional connotations,
in particular, its connection with the future:

> Qui? quoy? comment? a qui? pourquoy?
> Passez, presens ou avenir,
> Quant me viennent en souvenir
> Mon cueur en penser n'est pas coy.
> *(Poésies*, vol. 2, rondeau 300)

[Who? What? How? To whom? Why? Past, present, or future, when they come into my mind the thought disquiets my heart.]

The change was complete in the formulation we find in René d'Anjou's *Le Livre du Cuer d'Amours espris.* In his description of the fifth tapestry in the Hall of Love, the one dedicated to Souvenir, René states:

> Nommé suys Souvenir, avec Pensee aussi,
> Qui forgeons sans cesser, comme voyez icy,
> Fleurectes d'ancolies et soucïes tousjours
> Sur l'enclume de paine, de marteaulx de labours,
> Pour aux dolans amans qu'ont dames sont mercy
> Faire des chappelez avec fleurs de rebours.   (176)

> [My name is Memory, and together with Thought, we ceaselessly forge, as you see here, little flowers of melancholy «columbines» and cares «marigolds» on the anvil of sorrow with hammers of labor, to make crowns out of the flowers of regret for lovers with merciless ladies.]

Souvenir has left the sphere of the imagination that it previously occupied to enter into the sphere of memory proper. Writing took advantage of the void. Rather than playing with death, it was now death who was doing the playing—and the dancing and the acting. Insofar as we know, the theme of the *danse macabre* does not go back beyond 1400. The theme of the false death so dear to romance fantasy disappears. No one comes back out of the tomb any more, as in *Cligès;* they go into it. People are no longer intent on saving their bodies; they all attempt, in a number of ways, to preserve their names—better, their renown. No longer prophetic, the cemetery becomes didactic.

The cemeteries offered in literature are primarily places devoted to love. From places for the death and burial of individual lovers, they pass on to becoming cemeteries of Love in the abstract. Christine de Pizan wryly touches on this theme in *Le Debat de deux amans,* a work that dates from the early 1400s. A mournful knight has just listed the woes of love, and a skeptical lady responds:

> Je croy, par saint Nycaise!
> Qu'homme vivant n'est, a nul n'en desplaise,
>   Qui peust porter,
> Tans soit il fort, les maulz que raconter
> Vous oy yci, sanz la mort en gouster;
> Mais je n'ay point ou sont ouÿ conter
>   Ly cymentiere
> Ou enfouÿ sont ceulz qu'amours entiere
> A mis a mort, et qui por tel matiere
> Ont jeu au lit ou porté en litiere
>   Soient au saint
> Dont le mal vient; et quoy que dient maint
> Je croy que nul, fors a son aise, n'aint.
>
> (*Oeuvres poétiques,* vol. 2, ll. 982–94)

[I believe, by St. Nicasius, that—may it displease no one— no man ever lived strong enough to bear, without succumbing, the torments that I have heard you tell of here; and I have not heard speak of cemeteries in which those killed by a perfect love are buried, or who, for that reason, had to take to their beds or be carried on a litter to the saint from whom the sickness came; and in spite of what people say, I think that no one loves except for his pleasure.]

Christine de Pizan points the way, and we can trace the crystallization of the theme of the cemetery of Love through the enumerations of exempla of unhappy lovers who died for love or because of their love: Paris, Pyramus, Leander, Achilles, and Tristram but also Oenone, Thisbe, Dido, Iseult, and the Châtelaine de Vergi. Such lists were frequent. Christine's *Debat de deux amans* bears quite a complete one. Such examples were cited, one after the other, as arguments either for or against love and for or against women. *La Cruelle Femme en amour,* by Achille Caulier, a text written around 1430 by an author in the sphere of influence of Alain Chartier's *La Belle Dame sans mercy,* offers further confirmation. Caulier was one of the first authors to present this sort of cemetery of love. We are in a dream. The narrator has just visited the Temple of Venus. He states:

> Quant faitte euz ma pensee entiere,
> Je suy hors du temple passez
> Et entré ens ou cementiere
> Ou gisoient les trespassez.
> Par les tombes cogneux assez
> De ceulx qui gisoyent en terre,
> Qui onques ne furent lassez
> D'amer lealment sans meffaire.
>
> Je y cogneuz Helaine et Paris.   (Stanzas 27–28, ll. 209–17)

[After that thought, I left the temple and went into the cemetery where the dead lay. Among the tombs of those who were buried I recognized many who never tired of loving faithfully, doing no harm. I recognized Helen and Paris.]

Achille Caulier used the same formula in his *Hôpital d'Amour,* a work cited by Martin Le Franc and René d'Anjou.

What does it mean when an enumeration of tombs replaces a list of names? First, it is a sign of spatialization and shows a shift from the abstract to the concrete; next, it indicates a transfer from speech to vision and from ordinary writing to monumental writing. Didacticism is funneled through the picture and imagination of place. The stroll through the cemetery, stopping at the base of each monument, becomes analogous to a stroll through a monumentalized memory, a technique taught by the many works of the age on the arts of memory.

A dozen years later, Martin Le Franc refined the cemetery walk in his *Champion des dames.* Pursuing the possibilities that the spatial allegory offered, he has his hero, Franc Vouloir (Candor), visit both the Castle of Love and the Castle of Venus and compare the two castles, their cemeteries in particular. The cemetery of the Castle of Love appears as a melancholy version of the *locus amoenus,* Paradise:

> Du pré tout couvert de blans marbres,
> Semé de flours tresoudourans

> Et umbroyé de haults vers arbres,
> L'encens et le balsme flairans
>
> . . . .
>
> Tantost departismes.   (Ll. 1937–40, 1943)

[From the meadow covered with white marble «tombs», sown with sweet-smelling flowers, shaded by tall green trees, and smelling of balm and incense, . . . we soon departed.]

The cemetery of the Castle of Venus was the inverse of the *locus amoenus* and an antechamber of Hell:

> Tant alasmes en regardant
> Celuy cymentiere piteux
> Que nous venons au trou ardant,
> Au trou horrible et despiteux.   (Ll. 1361–64)

[We walked so far, observing the while, in that cemetery that fills one with pity, that we arrived at the flaming hole, at the horrible and hideous hole.]

Here the laments of souls in torment replace the song of the birds. "Les haults vers arbres" that reached up toward the sky give way to rampant plants—old moss, thorny bushes (ll. 1347–48)—that conceal what lies under them. The architectural, which, in the positive version, was a possible variant on the floral, disappears under a hostile vegetation. The tomb no longer fulfills its function of preserving the name. The cemetery is no longer a place of memory but one of dishonor and oblivion. The cemetery of Love, on the other hand, is related to art, as art was conceived at the time. In it, writing is a substitute for the voice, and lyric poetry, following the old aesthetic, was a joyous crystallization of the lament. The chapels there were

> plaines de dictiers gracieux
> Et de rondeaulx en lieu de plaintes
> Pour amuser les amoureux.   (Ll. 1990–92)

[full of graceful tales and rondeaus, not laments, to amuse lovers.]

The cemetery of love reached its full development with René d'Anjou in his *Livre du Cuer d'Amours espris*. Here it is not just unhappy and famous lovers who are celebrated but poets—masters of rhetoric and of the theory of love, master writers on love. The *grand et plantureux* (large and luxurious) cemetery becomes a library in René d'Anjou (141). The cemetery contains six tombs "non pas loign des autres mais comme mises a part et environnees de mur pour plusgrant excellence et espicialité, lesquelles estoient en nombre jucques a six et non plus" [not far from the others, but set apart and surrounded with a wall to mark their greater excellence and particularity, which were six in number and no more]. These were the tombs of Ovid, Guillaume de Machaut, Boccaccio, Jean de Meun, Petrarch, and Alain Chartier—a prestigious anthology!

It is obvious that this formulation owes much to the model of the pilgrimage—to Guillaume de Digulleville and his *Pèlerinage de la vie humaine, Pèlerinage de l'âme,* and *Pèlerinage de Jésus-Christ* and especially to Dante and *The Divine Comedy,* which Martin Le Franc cites in *Le Champion des dames.* The promenade, like the pilgrimage, allows the subject to invent places and occupy them. It encourages geographic imagination. With the pilgrimage, however, the subject is an actor; he advances on the right road. With the promenade, he is a spectator, a witness, an onlooking eye, a note-taking hand. The promenade in a cemetery—a less teleological activity than the pilgrimage—was better suited to the sentiments of an age that thought less of the salvation of its soul than of the survival of its name.

If a list of unhappy lovers generated the cemetery of love, a spatial variant of the temporal *ubi sunt,* the same could be said of all the other enumerations of famous men and women for which writers of the age showed such fondness. As we have seen with their treatment of Cadmus and Carmentis, the device enabled authors to inscribe their own names in the genealogy of their dreams or to escape a filiation they rejected. It was a new form of genealogy based on passing on a name (more accurately, a renown) rather than on blood. This was the age when the lists of the Nine Worthies, male and female (*les neuf preux* and *les neuf preuses*), crystallized and when enumerations of famous men and women sprang up everywhere in imitation of

Boccaccio's *De casibus virorum illustrium* and his *De mulieribus claris,* works that were translated several times and frequently borrowed from. The age loved lists. These appeared in inventories (real or imaginary) of one's library, in testaments (a coded form of the inventory), and in fictitious probate inventories such as the *Inventaire des biens demourez du decés de l'amant trespassé de dueil* by Pierre de Hauteville, the prince of the Cour d'Amour, a sequel to his *Confession et testament de l'amant trespassé de deuil.* We read there:

> La fut trouvé ung cartulat
> En françois rond sans quelque gloze,
> Le livre *Lancelot du Lac*
> Et ung vielz *Rommant de la Rose*
>
> . . . .
>
> Le livre des *Joies et Doulours*
> Du Jenne Amoureux Sans Soucy,
> La Belle Dame Sans Mercy
> Et aussi l'*Ospital d'Amours;*
>
> Passe temps Michault y estoit,
> L'Amoureux rendu cordelier
> Et d'autres livres ung millier
> Ou le Defunct si s'esbatoit.   (Ll. 429–32, 437–44)

[There was found a charter in simple French, with no gloss, the book of *Lancelot du Lac* and an old *Roman de la Rose,* . . . the book of the *Joies et douleurs du jeune amoureux sans souci, La Belle Dame sans mercy* and also *L'Hôpital d'Amour; Le Passe Temps* of Michault was found there, *L'Amoureux rendu cordelier,* and a thousand other books in which the deceased took pleasure.]

The cemetery was a privileged place for the spatial realization of such lists. Two systems of images met on that terrain, both of which made use of space and vision. The first was an imagery of conquest: cities were built on names. This was what Christine de Pizan did in *Le Livre de la cité des dames.* The second imagery was nostalgic: those same names (or others) could be contemplated written on tombstones. In Georges Chastelain's *Le Temple Bocace,* a work written in

1465, the author, lost in thought toward dawn ("entroublié ung peu envers l'aube du jour"; 7, ll. 4–5), begins to have a vision. A voice calls to him: "En vertu de la voix, je me trouvay, ne sçay comment, en ung cimitere plain de tombes" (9, ll. 5–6) [By the power of the voice, I found myself, I know not how, in a cemetery full of tombs].

As the author walks by one tomb after another, he sees passing before his eyes the whole of universal history from the Assyrians to the French. He himself is passive; he is pure gaze. His role is to register and to bear witness by writing, an act that duplicates, *en abyme,* the gaze of the original compiler. The nameless voice speaks to the *acteur* (the author) at the end of the book:

> O George . . . En ensievant doncques la nature du cas et dont tu es seul secretaire, seul auditeur et le seul ycy choisy, affin que la memoire n'en perisse et que ta vision peust autre part donner fruit, il te enjoint que tu le mettras par escript et que, toy riglant selon la retencion que tu en as et dont on se confie en toy, tu [le] publies par les royales cours et ailleurs, la ou il porra servir.
>
> (193, ll. 8, 10–16)

> [O Georges! . . . By thus following the nature of the case, of whose secret you are the sole scribe, the sole audience, the only one chosen here so that memory of it not die and so that your vision may bear fruit, it is your duty to put it into writing, letting yourself be guided by what you remember and what has been confided to you, and to publish it in the royal courts and elsewhere where it can be of service.]

In the 1500s, Antitus, the chaplain of the prince-bishop of Lausanne, Aymé de Montfalcon, returned to Georges Chastelain's work and continued it under the guise (as its title indicates) of a *Portail du temple de Bocace.* In the cemetery of memory Antitus includes recent dead who had been close to his bishop:

> Du temple fut Bocace fondateur,
> Le collecteur d'histoires anciennes,
> Du cymitire premier instituteur,
> Messire George.   (*Poésies,* 53, ll. 41–44)

[Boccaccio, who gathered together ancient histories, was the founder of the temple; the one who first instituted the cemetery is Mylord Georges.]

The literary cemeteries had a totally different moral purpose from the real cemeteries of the age, as historians have reconstructed them. The historical cemetery offered a lesson in humility and equality in which the dead rapidly disappeared; it spoke only of death. We can see this in the justly famous Cemetery of the Innocents in Paris. Jean Meschinot tells us in *Les Lunettes des princes,* speaking in the person of Justice:

> Si tu vas a Saint-Innocent
> Ou il y a d'ossement grant tas,
> Ja ne congnoistras entre cent
> Les os des gens des grans estas
> D'avec ceulx qu'au monde notas
> En leur vivant, povres et nus:
> Les corps vont dont ilz sont venuz. (Ll. 733–39)

[If you go the the Holy Innocents, where there are heaps of bones, you will not distinguish, in a hundred, the bones of the people of high estate from those who, in their lifetimes, were poor and naked: bodies return from whence they came.]

As Emile Mâle reminds us, "At this time there was perfect equality among the dead: the rich did not have [magnificent] houses in the cemetery, as they do today. When the time came, their grave was sold and their bones taken to the charnel house that stood above the cloister" (*Religious Art in France in the Late Middle Ages,* 329). François Villon delivers the same message in *Le Testament:*

> Quant je considere ces testes
> Entassees en ces charniers,
> Tous furent maistres des Requestes,
> Au moins de la Chambre aux deniers,
> Ou tous furent portepaniers;
> Autant puis l'un que l'autre dire,
> Car d'evesques ou lanterniers,
> Je n'y congnois riens a reddire. (Octave 162, ll. 1744–51)

[When I think of all those skulls heaped up in charnel houses, all once were Masters of Requests in the Royal Treasury at least, or perhaps just simple porters; I do not know which one is which. I can no longer tell you who was a bishop or a lantern-maker (Bonner translation, 115).]

In contrast with real cemeteries, the cemetery of memory offered a lesson on pride, or at least on the will to survive by glory. It was a trace of one's self beyond the tomb.

The representation of the cemetery was related to the representation of memory and of the book. All three were thought of as receptacles—englobing, containing places—in a subtle dialectic of opening and closing, no longer by force but by reading. All three are presented as like tablets to be deciphered. This is the underlying reason for René d'Anjou's insistence on noting the types of letters in which the epitaphs in his cemetery of Love in the *Livre du Cuer d'Amour espris* are written: they are "en lectres et langaige romain" (121) [in Roman letters and in Latin] for the tomb of Julius Caesar; "en ancienne lectre lombarde" (122) [in ancient Lombard letters] for the tomb of Augustus; and "lectres en ebreu escriptes" (124) [written in Hebrew letters] for the tomb of David (though all inscriptions were also given in French translation).

The reasons for this lay deeper than René's antiquarian tastes. The epitaphs on the white tombstones were to be read like the characters blackening the white pages of books. The cemetery, the memory, and the book fulfilled the same function of remembrance. All of them contained a discontinuous series of objects, scattered bits to be both remembered and re-membered—*rememorare* and *remembrare.* One could combat the decomposition of the body (which Eustache Deschamps called "worms' meat"—*viande pour les vers*—in the refrain of a ballade [*Oeuvres complètes,* 1:240–41, no. 120] through the marble of the tomb. One could resist the dissolution of *souvenir* by the faculty of memory, which recalls—*recorde*—and one could stave off oblivion and dispersion by means of the book, which reconstructs—*re-corde* —taking up the loose threads and braiding them into a crown or a chaplet. This play on words (anagram is a frequent device in these texts) is the perfect *mise en abyme* of the dual movement that disassembles in order to reassemble, that dismembers and re-members names. Memory pulsates. To write was to "coucher par écrit" [lay down in writing]. Writing becomes a tomb; there is a will to survive both by leaving a trace and by compelling others to read what is dictated.

In a familiar passage at the end of the *Phaedrus,* Plato gives expression to the Greeks' scorn for writing and for the book. King Thamus refuses Theuth's offer of his new invention, the alphabet: "It will implant forgetfulness in [men's] souls: they will cease to exercise memory. . . . It is no true wisdom that you offer your disciples, but only its semblance" (*Phaedrus,* 274e, Hackforth translation, 157).

Petrarch recalls the proper use of the book in *De remediis utriusque fortunae:* "If you want glory from your books, you must take another road: not just have them but know them; not place them in your library but in your memory; and lock them in your mind and not in your bookcase. Otherwise, nobody would be more famous than the public bookseller or the bookstall itself" ("On the Abundance of Books," Rawski translation, 43)

What was the significance of the new link between memory and the book, which were thought of in homological terms at the end of the Middle Ages? The connection signaled a choice between possible means of perpetuation. It set up a parallel between reproduction by lineage—by sexual engendering—which was the business of nobles, and reproduction by the book, which was the business of the clerks. We see here one more episode in the rivalry between the clerk and the knight to which debates, first in Latin, then in French, had borne witness for centuries. The arguments for both sides were summarized admirably by Eustache Deschamps in his *Miroir de mariage.* Here is his argument in favor of marriage, or survival through lineage:

> Et donques par plus fort raison,
> Tu, qui es raisonnables hom
> Et qui as ame intellective
> Perpetuel, saige et soubtive
> Doiz mieulx tendre a avoir lignée

Par le moien d'espouse née
Que tu deusses prandre et henter
Pour ta forme representer,
Toy et ton nom après la mort
Selon la loy.

(*Oeuvres complètes*, 9:9–10, no. 1498, ll. 189–98)

[And hence, for even greater reason, you who are a reason-
able man and who have an intelligent soul, eternal, wise,
and subtle, you must try even harder to found a lineage by
means of a wife whom you should take and know in order
to safeguard your form and your name after death, according to the law.]

Lineage was memory. What should one do, then, if one was noble
and had no children? Found a city, following the example of Epaminondas cited by Christine de Pizan in her *Livre du corps de policie*.

The argument against marriage was survival by the book. For although perpetuation was possible through "memoire par trois choses"
(*Miroir de mariage*, 9:260, ll. 8022–23) [memory by three things]—
valor, knowledge, and the construction of cities—in the last analysis
it all came down to writing: "tout se ramaine a escript" (l. 8024).

Ancor n'ara tant travillié
Chevaliers ne li clers villé,
Se leurs fais n'estoient escrips,
Si com j'ay leu en mains escrips,
Figurez ou mis en painture,
Qui tout revient a escripture,
Ou taillez de pierre de taille,
Comme on figure une bataille,
Ou comme l'en fait voulentiers
Les ymaiges en ces moustiers
Des vierges, des sains et des sainctes.

(9:259, ll. 7995–8005)

[The knight will have taken pains in vain and the clerk
made his vigil if their actions had not been written down, as
I have read in many works, represented, or painted (for
everything comes down to writing), or sculpted on cut

stone, as is done for a battle or as is often done in churches
in images of the Virgin and the saints, male and female.]

Memory had a relation to both generation and the book. This was
often expressed obliquely. Thus the word *armoire,* often used to designate memory, was also used to refer to the woman's "natural parts."
Similarly, the image of an impression or stamp was used for what is
registered in memory (*mémoire*) but also for what is engendered in
the womb (*matrice*). The parallel is explicit in Christine de Pizan,
who passes from *femme* (woman) to *fame* or *fama* (fame, renown).
These words were pronounced identically in the Middle Ages and
occasionally spelled the same, showing the triumph of the clerk and
the pride of the writer.

Jean Roudaut opens his *Autre Part: Paysages d'accompagnement*
with a magnificent decasyllable: "Je n'ai jamais écrit que des tombeaux" [I have never written anything but eulogies]. As the Middle
Ages drew to a close, the voice was abandoned for the book; things
warm and palpitating were replaced by marble, the bird by the tomb.
This would have been a perfect epitaph to crown its disenchantment
and seal its self-communion. *Tombeaux?* If we think of Petrarch, we
might as easily say triumphs.

6 | *Companions in Verse, Wine, and Spirit*

One way to interpret fourteenth-century literature is through a vertical network of fathers, filiation, and the engendering of matter. Another is by looking at the horizontal network of companions. Here the author no longer places himself solely within a lineage—the lineage of inventors, for example—but within a group of like-minded friends connected by shared pleasures and writing. Brotherhoods became literary as well as chivalric; writers passed, as it were, from *pères* (fathers) to *pairs* (peers).

That horizontal network developed in two ways. First, there were joyous confraternities, bacchic and goliardic companies, the network *in praesentia* of friends with whom one had a good time; second, there was the network of serious-minded companies and humanist circles, the *in absentia* network of the friends to whom one wrote. Companionship took a number of forms, and it demonstrated immense literary vitality, a taste for writing, and pleasure taken in literature.

The first of these networks operated under the sign of joy and wine. Joyous drinkers and merry fellows gathered as *galois* and the *frequentans* of the taverns. We see them in the *Charte des bons enfans de Vertus en Champaigne* written by Eustache Deschamps and dated August 1372:

Le souverain des Frequentans,
Qui sa vie a usé cent ans
A suir taverne a Vertus,
Bien gouvernez et mal vestus,
A touz les enfans de la ville
Qui a frequenter sont habile,

. . . .

Salut!   (*Oeuvres complètes,* 7:323, no. 1400, ll. 1–6, 10)

[The king of the bon vivants who spent a hundred years of
his life frequenting the taverns of Vertus, well guided and
poorly dressed, to all the children of the town who like to
frequent ill-famed places, . . . Greetings!]

Galois and *gais lurons* (merry fellows) were present throughout the
fourteenth and fifteenth centuries. We meet them in Gilles Li Muisis. In *La Complainte des compagnons,* Campions hails Gilles with
"Vous fustes cancelier dou prince de le Gale" (*Poésies,* 2:261, l. 17)
[You were chancellor to the prince of the Merry Fellows], and Gilles
responds, "Le prince de le Gale je siervi loyalment" (2:266, l. 2) [I
faithfully served the prince of the Merry Fellows].

The *gentils Galois* wept for Guillaume de Machaut in the double
ballade that Eustache Deschamps composed for his master's death:
"Faictes devoir, plourez, gentils Galois" (1:246, no. 124, l. 23) [Do
your duty and weep, gentle merrymakers]. This line echoes, in another tone of voice, the "Vestez vous noir, plourez, tous, Cham-
penois" (1:244, no. 123, l. 23) [Dress yourselves in black and weep, all
you from Champagne] of the first ballade.

Geoffrey Chaucer read his own name as *Galfriedus,* or "friend of
gaity." We find *galois* in Jean Froissart's *Chroniques* and *compains de
galle* in François Villon's *Testament:*

A vous parle, compains de galle,
Mal des ames et bien du corps.   (Ll. 1720–21)

[To you I speak, my friends with whom I had good times,
whose souls are sick and bodies well (Bonner translation,
113).]

François Villon even devoted an entire ballade to his pleasure-loving friends, *La Ballade de bonne doctrine* (*Le Testament*, ll. 1692–1719), whose refrain is much to the point: "Tout aux tavernes et aux filles" [All to the girls and the taverns (Bonner translation, 111)].

In his old age, the Chevalier de La Tour Landry recalled the times of his youth when he rode with companions who begged love from countless *dames* and *demoiselles*, "tant estoyent beaux langagiers et emparlez" (*Le Livre du Chevalier de La Tour Landry*, 3) [so fine and so easy was their speech].

Wine entered into the definition of the poet and of poetry in two ways. First, it allowed the poet to create his persona as a jongleur, a humble, amused pose miming a condition that in reality he had left behind. The poet presented himself as ugly, even afflicted with a serious physical defect—Guillaume de Machaut and Jean Molinet were blind in one eye, Eustache Deschamps was bald (close-cropped hair was one sign of insanity), Jean Le Fèvre limped. All of these authors, who declare their particular fondness for wine, present themselves as ugly and as poets. Eustache Deschamps gleefully proclaims himself "le roy des Lays" (4:274, no. 774, refrain) [the king of the ugly men]. Jean Molinet speaks of himself as "le maire des letz" (*Les Faicts et dictz*, 1:400, l. 28) [chief among the ugly].

Going one another one better was characteristic of the later generations, and we can catch them slyly referring to other poets. Jean Molinet says of himself, "Moy borgne d'oeul et le maire des letz" [Me, blind in one eye and chief among the ugly], a reference not only to Eustache Deschamps but also to another poet, Jean Lemaire de Belges, who was a relative of Molinet's. Eustache Deschamps may have been king of the *laids* but he was also king of *lais,* as his *Art de dictier* demonstrates: "Et de ceste musique naturele . . . vueil je traictier principaument, en baillant et enseignant un petit de regle ci après declarée a ceuls que nature avra encliné ou enclinera a ceste naturele musique, afin que ilz saichent congnoistre les façons et couples des *lais*" (*Oeuvres complètes*, 7:272, ll. 1396) [And of that natural music «poetry» . . . I want to treat in particular by giving and teaching a small group of rules, which I expose below, to those whom nature has inclined or will incline to that natural music, so that they may know how to make the stanzas of lays].

But wine, ugliness, and poetry made the poet a divine figure as well as a grotesque one, because he was a reflection of Bacchus, whom Eustache Deschamps called "Bacchus, poete divin" (8:70, no. 1420, l. 93) and "ce hault poete divin / Bachus" (8:103, no. 1437, ll. 18–19). The pun *de vin / divin* coupled wine and divinity on a profound level. In Guillaume de Machaut's *Le Dit de la harpe,* it is Orpheus who is called *poëte devin*:

> Quant Orpheüs le poëte devin
> Fit sacrefice ou il n'ot point de vin.   (Ll. 31–32)

> [When Orpheus, the divine poet, made a sacrifice without wine.]

The poet occupied a space somewhere between an Orpheus figure and a Bacchus figure; a figure of harmony and one of disorder and lack of measure, especially of sexual imbalance (sexual excess or deficiency). Eustache Deschamps plays ceaselessly—and Jean Molinet after him—with setting up parallels between the vocabulary of the sex act and the vocabulary of literary creation. Words such as *oeuvre* (work) and *besogne* (task) functioned on both levels. This produced strange echoes. The *Ovide moralisé* depicts Silenus (in the company of Priapus) at the wedding feast of Thetis and Peleus:

> A ces noces fu Silenus,
> Li viellars yvrais, qui but tant
> Que le vin aloit sangloutant
> Et vomissant parmi la bouche
> Si ne se mut plus c'une couche.
>   (Vol. 4, bk. 11, ll. 1284–88)

> [Silenus was at the wedding feast, the drunken oldster, who drank so much that he coughed up wine, vomited it from his mouth, and moved no more than a stump.]

Tears were not the only consequence of drinking wine. This passage was echoed by Guillaume de Machaut in *La Fonteinne amoureuse,* where Guillaume omits Silenus but presents Priapus "o sa

perche / Qui sa robe lieve et reverche" (ll. 1675–76) [with his erection,
who lifted up his robe and peeked (Palmer translation, 179)]. We read
in the *Voir-Dit,* however:

> Amours ne m'amoit, ne je li,
> Ainçois rassambloie à celi
> Qu'on compere à une viés souche.   (Ll. 735–37)

> [Love did not love me and I did not love it either; to the
> contrary, I resembled the one compared to an old stump.]

Was the aging poet prey to a melancholy that distanced him from
love, seeing himself as a grotesque Silenus, the *vieillard yvrais* of the
Ovide moralisé? Indirect echoes operate thanks to the rhyme. Eustache Deschamps links the vapors of wine

> dont le cervel est enfumé
> Et pluseurs en sont enrumé
>   (*Oeuvres complètes,* 7:324, no. 1400, ll. 25–26)

> [that cloud the brain and make some people catch a cold]

to the vapors of melancholy and of poetry. He creates the order of
the Fumeux (the inebriated):

> Jehan Fumée, par la grace du monde
> Ou tous baras et tricherie habonde,
> Empereres et sires des Fumeux,
> Et palatins des Merencolieux,
> A tous baillis, prevosts et seneschaulx,
>
> . . . .
>
> Amour, salut avec dilection!   (7:312, no. 1398, ll. 1–5, 14

> [John Vapors, by the grace of the world in which falsity and
> trickery abound, emperor and lord of the Vaporous and the
> defenders of the Melancholy, to all bailiffs, provosts, and
> seneschals, . . . love and health!]

For the clerk-poets there was a connection between wine and the
book. A florin as *contrefait* (counterfeit; badly made) as the poet,
which has not been spent because it does not look just right, tots up
the expenditures of its owner, Jean Froissart:

Tout premiers, vous avés fait livres
Qui ont cousté bien .VII.c livres.
L'argent avés vous mis la bien;
Je le prise sus toute rien,
Car fait en avés mainte hystore
Dont il sera encore memore
De vous ens ou temps a venir.

. . . .

Et les tavreniers de Lestines,
Entroes que la vous ordeniés
Et que la cure gouvreniés,
En ont bien eü cinq cens frans.

> (*Le Dit dou florin,* in *"Dits" et "Débats,"*
> 181, ll. 199–205, 208–11)

[First of all, you made books that cost a good seven hundred
pounds. In that you invested your money well. I appreciate
that investment above all others, for you made many stories
by which you will be remembered in times to come. . . .
And the tavern keepers of Estinnes-au-Mont, while you
were composing there and were the parish priest, had a
good five hundred francs.]

According to the florin, the third reason for Jean Froissart's poverty
was his travels. Wine, writing, and voyages drew a new landscape of
the literary imagination in the fourteenth century.

The horizontal network of companions might also be a learned company struggling, in bitter or friendly combat, for mastery of their
craft or for literary recognition. Petrarch's quarrel with the French humanists Anseau Choquart and Jean de Hesdin is a familiar story: Petrarch had stated, "Extra Italiam oratores et poetas non querendos"
(Petrarca, *Rerum senilium* 9.1) [Orators and poets are not to be found
outside Italy (Bernardo, Levin, and Bernardo translation, 1:312)]. An
exchange of ballades (in French rather than Latin this time) toward
the middle of the century among Philippe de Vitry, Jean de Le Mote,
and Jean Campion introduced a way of speaking about poetry that
was tinged with mythology and celebrated the inspiration of the

Muses. Philippe de Vitry accused Jean de Le Mote of not knowing how to make Pegasus fly: "tu, qui ne vaulz une mite / A Pegasus faire voler":

> Certes, Jehan, la fons Cirree
> Ne te congnoit, ne li lieux vers
> Ou maint la vois Caliopee.
> Car amoureus diz fais couvers
> De nons divers.
> (Diekstra, "The Poetic Exchange," 508, ll. 25–26, 19–23)

[Indeed, John, the fountain of Cirrha does not know you, nor the green place where the voice of Calliope stays. For you make amorous poems filled with divers names (Diekstra translation, 510).]

Jean de Le Mote responded in highly respectful terms:

> O Victriens, mondains Dieu d'armonie,
> Filz Musicans et per a Orpheus,
> Supernasor de la fontaine Helye,
>
> . . . .
>
> Car en la fons Cirree est tes escus.   (Ibid., 509, ll. 1–3, 15)

[O man of Vitry, worldly god of harmony, son of Musicans and peer of Orpheus, Superlative Naso «Ovid» of the fountain of Helicon, . . . your escutcheon is on the fountain of Cirrha (Diekstra translation, 510–11).]

The *fons Cirree,* the fountain and spring of the Muses on Mount Helicon, can also be found in a ballade by Eustache Deschamps, composed on the occasion of the death of Guillaume de Machaut. The scribe who copied it did not understand the mention of *Cirrée,* putting *Circé* in its stead:

> La fons Circé et la fontaine Helie
> Dont vous estiez le ruissel et les dois.
> (*Oeuvres complètes,* 1:245, no. 124, ll. 9–10)

[The fountain of «Cirrha» and the fountain of the Helicon, whose stream and conduits you were.]

In another ballade, Eustache Deschamps deplores the theft of one of his manuscripts in these terms:

> Doulz Zephirus qui faiz naistre les flours,
> Printemps, Esté, Autompne, et Aurora,
> Plourez o moy mes dolentes dolours
> Et le jardin que jadis laboura
> Fons Cireus, ou Galiope ouvra,
> Qui de ses fleurs avoit fait un chapel.
>
> (5:229, no. 984, ll. 1–6)

> [Sweet Zephyr, you who bring the flowers to birth, Spring, Summer, Autumn, and Dawn, weep with me over my painful woes, and for the garden once watered by the fountain of Cirrha, where Calliope worked and of its flowers made a crown.]

The book, then, was a garden watered by the fountain of the Muses.

The fountain of Cirrha appears again in the invocation that opens Chaucer's *Compleynte of Faire Anelida and False Arcite,* "On Párnaso . . . by Elicon, not fer from Cirreá" (*Works,* 304, l. 18).

A dense and busy network of literary exchanges sprang up throughout Europe. Eustache Deschamps addressed a ballade to Geoffrey Chaucer, "d'amours mondains Dieux en Albie" (l. 12) [the god of worldly love in England]:

> A toy pour ce de la fontaine Helye
> Requier avoir un buvraige autentique.
>
> (2:139, no. 285, ll. 22–23)

> [For that reason, I ask you for an authentic draught from the fountain of the Helicon.]

Christine de Pizan sent an *Epistre* to Eustache Deschamps, "orateur de maint vers notable" (l. 4) [orator of many a notable line], dated 10 February 1403 (*Oeuvres poétiques,* 2:295–301). She calls him "chier maistre et amis" (l. 6) [dear master and friend], "chier frere et amy" (l. 163) [dear brother and friend], and she calls herself "ta disciple et ta bienveillant" (l. 212) [your disciple and well-wisher], showing that theirs was a connection of reverence but also of friendship.

She begs Eustache to excuse her for using the familiar "tu" with him, but that, she states, was the custom in correspondence among literary folk (ll. 18–22). Eustache answered Christine, paying her the supreme compliment of comparing her to a muse: "Muse eloquent entre les .IX., Christine" (*Oeuvres complètes,* 6:251, no. 1242, l. 1) [Muse most eloquent among the nine, Christine]. The friendship network broadens in the envoi:

> O douce suer, je, Eustace, te prie,
> Comme ton serf, d'estre en ta compaignie
> Pour bien avoir d'estude congnoissance;
> Mieulx en vaudray tous les temps de ma vie,
> Car je te voy, com Boece a Pavie,
> Seule en tes faiz au royaume de France.   (6:252, ll. 31–36)

> [O sweet sister, I, Eustache, as your servant I beg you to receive me in your company so that I may know study well; I will become the better for it for all my life, for I see you, like Boethius at Pavia, unique in your actions in the kingdom of France.]

Philippe de Mézières, who was a friend of Petrarch's and who had spent three years in Venice, translated into French the Latin version (by Petrarch) of the story of Griselda, the last novella in Boccaccio's *Decameron.* As tutor to the young Charles VI, Philippe set up a reading program for the young king, and Eustache Deschamps was one of the contemporary authors whom he recommended. Philippe states, speaking through Reine Vérité (Queen Truth): "Tu puez bien lire aussi et ouyr les dictez vertueulx de ton serviteur et officier Eustache Morel, et toutes autres escriptures vrayes, honnestes et catholiques, tendans a bonne edification" (*Le Songe du vieil pelerin,* 2:223) [You can also read and listen to the moral compositions of your servant and official Eustache Morel «Eustache Deschamps», and any other true, honest, and Catholic writing that leads to proper edification].

There were places and milieus specially dedicated to books: Paris and the *librairie* (library) of the Louvre, with Gilles Malet, a friend of Christine de Pizan's; the Collège de Navarre, whose great "master" was Nicole Oresme; Avignon and the popes; Constance at the time of the councils. Avignon, for example, had as residents or visitors Nicolas Trevet, Marsilius of Padua, Pierre Bersuire, William of Occam, Jean de Jandun, Philippe de Vitry, Richard de Bury, and, of course, Petrarch. There were bibliophiles: Richard de Bury, Petrarch, Boccaccio, Guillaume Fillastre. In his *Philobiblon*, Richard de Bury speaks of his "ecstatic" love (*hic amor exstaticus*) for books. Correspondence wove connections among these learned men and women. The love letter, a brilliant example of which was Guillaume de Machaut's *Voir-Dit*, gave way to letters between friends and colleagues. One of these exchanges was between Christine de Pizan and Jean de Montreuil and Pierre and Gontier Col, secretaries to the king, in the *querelle* about the *Roman de la Rose*; others were the letters of Jean Gerson, Jean Muret, Nicolas de Clamanges, and Pierre d'Ailly. A rhetoric of the epistle came into being, along with an aesthetic of fraternal collaboration.

Brothers appeared in literature: Petrarch and his brother Gherardo, a Carthusian monk; Jean Gerson and his brother Jean, a Celestine friar; Charles d'Orléans and his brother and companion in captivity, Jean d'Angoulême. Guillaume Alexis, a Norman monk, wrote a *Passetemps des deux Alecis freres* about his brother and himself. It would be interesting, in this connection, to follow the fortunes of Cicero's *De amicitia* (a work that Jean de Meun already knew from its rediscovery by the Florentine humanist Poggio Bracciolini). Nicolas de Clamanges made a copy of a version of Cicero's treatise (MS, Fonds latin 15138, Bibliothèque nationale, Paris). Laurent de Premierfait translated the same text in 1410, dedicating his translation to Louis, duc de Bourbon (MS, Fonds français 126, Bibliothèque nationale, Paris). At its rise in this period, creative friendship might be said to have reached its height in the dialogue between Montaigne and La Boétie.

7 A Century's Aged, Worn-out Children

Etienne Gilson once recalled, "Nothing was newer in its time than the scholastic method, nothing more modern; that was what the humanists of the next age detested in it. It is perhaps not often enough recognized that their well-known cult of Antiquity implied a complementary hatred of Modernity" ("Le Moyen Age comme *Saeculum Modernum*," 8). Basing his argument on an analysis of Filarete's *Trattato d'architettura*, Gilson shows that in his combat against what he disliked, Filarete always called modern what we today call medieval.

French poets at the end of the Middle Ages did not consider themselves modern. To the contrary, they often spoke of themselves as the worn-out, aged children of a century that was the last age of the world. As in Charles d'Orléans, they were aging schoolboys. This was also Jules Michelet's overall judgment of the Middle Ages. The age "naît avec des rides; c'est un vieil enfant à l'école qui épelle d'une voix cassée, peureux, tremblant entre le fouet et les férules" (*Journal*, 2:39) [was born wrinkled; it was an aged child at school, spelling with a broken voice, fear ridden, trembling between the whip and the rod]. Points of view are relative, as are ways of thinking about one's self or thinking about others. They differ according to whether they reflect ongoing present experience, which is always unique, or start from a retrospective, organizing, and demonstrative gaze.

The humanists operated on the period that preceded their own with brute force. They effected a massive reduction to unity that brought the Middle Ages down to one concept and one practice, scholasticism. What is more, they gave a pejorative interpretation to that unified concept, equating everything scholastic with pedantry. Did the humanists set themselves apart from scholasticism because they felt too close to it? Were there other reasons?

My intention in this study has been twofold: to reintroduce a degree of distinction into the period that the humanists considered and rejected globally in the interests of self-affirmation and, in particular, to emphasize a number of characteristic features of the last two centuries of the French Middle Ages with particular focus on forms and their meaning. Three linked changes seem to me essential to an understanding of these evolving forms. The first is the shift—which had begun long before—from the oral to the written. During the fourteenth century, the written vernacular reached all domains of knowledge. Latin lost its status as the language of God and his book, the Bible. This was a major desacralization. At a second stage, disenchantment set in—in lyric poetry, literally. Speech deserted the song, creating a dichotomy that had profound consequences. One of these was the custom of putting aside lyric poems for later use, an innovation of such importance that its possibilities were examined in a new narrative genre, the *dit,* a tale with lyrical insertions. Finally, poetic disenchantment was emblematic of a host of other sorts of disenchantment—with people, with the world—and it raised the question of harmony. Max Weber spoke of a disenchantment with the world, a process of secularization that began in those centuries and ended, according to Leo Spitzer, in the eighteenth century.

What about the "long fourteenth century"? That judgment can still be encountered today in the writings of historians weary of describing a period that seems to them a series of calamities. A tiresome fourteenth century, more boring than any other century? Perhaps. A long century? Yes, one might allow this, with a tinge of amusement, since it ended in the years between 1415 and 1418. The fourteenth century died at Agincourt in the spasms of the French defeat, the English occupation of France, and the civil war.

One of the earliest works of Alain Chartier, *Le Livre des quatre dames,* which dates from 1416, echoes that disaster. The poet, alone and melancholy because his lady does not return his love, is walking in the country. He encounters four ladies, each of whom laments her own misfortune born of the French defeat. The first lady's lover had died on the field of battle; the second's was taken prisoner. The third's had disappeared: was he dead? was he a prisoner? The lover of the fourth had fled. Which lady was the most unhappy? Chivalry had in fact been shattered at Agincourt. For proof, we need only look at the names of members of the Cour d'Amour listed in its charter who lost their lives there: Charles, seigneur d'Albret, connétable of France, for whom Christine de Pizan had written several ballades (in one of these she sends him as a gift *Le Debat de deux amans,* a work in which he is mentioned in flattering terms); Messire Guillaume de Melun, count of Tancarville; Jacques de Châtillon, admiral of France; Messire Jehan, seigneur de Werchin, sénéchal of Hainaut (whom Christine had often called upon to act as an arbiter of amorous questions, for example, at the beginning of the *Livre des trois jugements*); Antoine and Jean de Craon.

The list of the dead is impressive, and it continued. Charles d'Orléans was taken prisoner. Writers were killed in the troubles of the civil war. Jacques Legrand died in 1415; Gontier Col and Jean de Montreuil died in the massacres that accompanied the entry of the Burgundians into Paris in May 1418. Other writers left the city: Christine de Pizan, Jean Gerson, and Alain Chartier, who followed the dauphin. Intellectual circles were broken up and their members dispersed; libraries (Jean de Montreuil's, for example) were scattered or lost. Charles V's library was eventually bought, at the death of Charles VI, by the duke of Bedford, the regent for the kingdom. The last inventory, taken in 1424 for the appraisal of its holdings, shows that only 843 manuscripts were left.

Alain Chartier set up a new paradigm in the literary domain. He played the same role for authors of the fifteenth century that *Le Ro-*

man de la Rose had played for writers of the preceding period, in particular in the realms of love and of courtly ritual. *La Belle Dame sans mercy* was a text that prompted strong reactions on the part of some of the clergy, and there was a "quarrel" of *La Belle Dame sans mercy* just as there had been a "quarrel" of *Le Roman de la Rose* at the beginning of the fifteenth century. Writers passed judgment on the lady and took sides. Her statement that "les yeux sont faits pour regarder" (l. 238) [eyes are made for looking], which dealt a deadly blow to the courtly ethic, was echoed by a number of authors. "Les yeulz si sont fais pour servir," wrote Charles d'Orléans (*Poésies,* vol. 1, chanson 53) [eyes were created to serve (Spence translation, 109)], an inversion of Alain Chartier's formula in that it came from the mouth of a lover, not a lady.

For many writers, the lady's eyes were no longer a mirror of the other and of his desire; rather, they became an optical instrument. Alain Chartier was wily enough to leave the debate open, electing no judge. As a result, the entire fifteenth century slipped into that empty judge's seat. The first reaction to *La Belle Dame sans mercy* was a *Requeste envoyée par les amans aux dames contre Alain* in which the lovers reproached the poet for his "nouvellectez" (35, l. 21) [novelties]. Next came a *Lettre des dames,* a *Response des dames à maistre Alain,* and an entire series of texts studied in the early years of this century by Arthur Piaget: the *Parlement d'Amour* by Baudet Herenc, *La Dame loyale en amours* and *Cruelle femme en amour* by Achille Caulier, *Erreurs du jugement de la Belle Dame sans mercy, Belle Dame qui eut merci,* and others—the list was long.

When he created the figure of the Belle Dame, Alain Chartier moved the question of love onto a new terrain. With *Le Quadrilogue invectif* (1422) he renewed the very subject matter of writing by focusing on France as an object of reflection and love. In that prose text, Dame France appears to the poet in a morning dream in which she calls up the three orders, the People, the Knighthood, and the Clergy. France speaks first and last; the mother embraces and dominates the whole. Alain Chartier, "lointaing immitateur des orateurs" [late imitator of the orators], as he calls himself at the start of the

Quadrilogue invectif, inaugurated a type of rhetorical eloquence new to France.

For all these reasons, Alain Chartier became the writer to whom everyone referred at the end of the Middle Ages and the beginning of the sixteenth century; he was the model marking the start of a new epoch in French letters. Authors of "arts of rhetoric" cited him with admiration and borrowed many of his exempla. Taking over from the "sons" of the fourteenth century, Alain Chartier set himself up as a new "father." Indeed, later ages called him "the father of French eloquence," an expression that appears in Pierre Fabri's *Grant et vray art de pleine rhétorique* (1521): "O mort mortellement cruelle! pourquoy as tu pris maistre Alain Charetier, le pere de l'eloquence françoyse?" (1:72) [O death, mortally cruel! Why have you taken master Alain Chartier, the father of French eloquence?]. The same expression appears in Jean Bouchet's *Annales d'Aquitaine* (1524). Alain Chartier figures with Jean de Meun in the first canon of classical French authors to be compiled. Thomas Sébillet has this to say in his chapter on invention in *L'Art poétique français* (1548): "L'invention, et le jugement compris sous elle, se confirment et enrichissent par la lecture des bons et classiques poètes français comme sont entre les vieux Alain Chartier, et Jean de Meun" (59) [Invention and the judgment that is a part of it are confirmed and enriched by reading the good and classical French poets such as, among the older ones, Alain Chartier and Jean de Meun].

This study began with a reflection on the image of the Jubilee year pilgrimages to Rome that punctuated the century. The fourteenth century had a problem of orientation. All roads no longer led to Rome; for a good many years, some led to Avignon. Intellectual orientation shifted as well. The fourteenth century opened and closed with flaming pyres and with the image of women burning at the stake. On 1 June 1310, Marguerite Porete, who was connected with the Free Spirit movement, was burned alive as a heretic in the Place de Grève in Paris. Her one book, *Le Mirouer des simples ames anienties et qui seulement demourent en vouloir et desir d'amour,* had been condemned by the bishop of Cambrai and publicly burned at Valencienne in the presence of its author. On 29 May 1431, the woman for whom Christine de Pizan took up her pen again in 1429—Joan of Arc—was burned at the stake at Rouen.

The model that has served us throughout this study is that of the family. This simple and powerful schema clearly played a major role in medieval thought. There were various reasons for this, religious, historical, and anthropological. The Holy Family provided a model of a good son—Christ—and the Bible contained many examples of bad sons on the pattern of Satan or Adam. These "bad sons" became fathers fatal for their progeny. Man in general was a damned son redeemed by the death of a good son, Christ, who should be imitated. Eustache Deschamps recalls this in his *Double Lay: De la Nativité Nostre Seigneur* when he speaks of

> ceuls qui furent d'Adam nez,
> Qui estoient condempnez
> A mort par leurs ancessors.
> (*Oeuvres complètes*, 7:154, no. 1358, ll. 129–31)

> [those who were born of Adam and were condemned to death by their forebears.]

The rhyme *dampné* (damned) / *d'Adam né* (born of Adam) was frequent. Eustache Deschamps used it in his *Notable Dictié de Nostre Seigneur Jhesu Crist et de la Benoite Vierge Marie, sa douce Mere* (7:144, no. 1356, ll. 107–8).

The familial model made it possible for the Middle Ages to think about the moral life. Allegories of the vices and the virtues followed the family pattern, as did those of the psychic and intellectual categories of life. It provided a convenient mold that facilitated comprehension of categorization and transgression; it offered both horizontal and vertical lines, the *fils* (threads) and the *fils* (sons).

The book was seen as a child in the fourteenth century. It was *liber*. Authors played with the etymology of the word, which signified both "tree bark" and "son" (*liber* and *liberi*). A book was begotten; it was given a name—its title, over which the author had increasing control. The book had a voice. It was only in the fifteenth century that the book (at least in French) became autonomous, emancipated from its father, and able to speak for itself. As early as Richard de Bury's *Philobiblon,* books spoke out (in Latin) to reprimand the clerks who copied them inaccurately. Two scenes of an author offering his book to the sovereign make an interesting comparison. Toward the end of his life (in 1395), during his last trip to England, Jean Froissart offered a manuscript copy of his collected poems to King Richard II:

Il l'ouvry et regarda ens, et luy pleut très grandement et bien plaire luy devait, car il estoit enluminé, escript et historié et couvert de vermeil velours à dix clous attachiés d'argent dorés et roses d'or ou milieu, à deux grans frumaux dorés et richement ouvrés au milieu de roses d'or. Adont me demanda le roy de quoy il traittoit. Je luy dis: "D'amours." De ceste reponse fut-il tous resjouys, et regarda dedens le livre en plusieurs lieux et y lisy, car moult bien parloit et lisoit le franchois, et puis le fist prendre par ung sien chevallier qui se nommoit messire Richard Credon et porter en sa chambre de retraite, et me fist de plus en plus bonne chière et bon recueillotte à merveilles.   (*Chroniques,* vol. 15, bk. 4, p. 167)

[He opened it and read it with considerable pleasure, as well he might, for it was beautifully written and illuminated, and bound in crimson velvet with ten silver-gilt studs, and roses embroidered in gold in the centre. The King asked the subject of my poems and I replied that they were concerning love. The King was delighted, and read out several of the poems, for he read and spoke French fluently. He then handed it to one of his knights, Sir Richard Credon, and told him to put it in his private «quarters». The King was most affable to me about the book (Jolliffe translation, 362).]

When Martin Le Franc arranged to have his *Champion des dames* offered to Philippe le Bon around 1442, the work met with a quite different reception. The duke deigned to touch the book,

> D'honneur m'a fait plus que ne vaulx,
> Car il m'a touchié de sa main,
> > (*Complainte du livre du champion des dames a maistre Martin Le Franc son acteur,* ll. 129-30)

> [He did me more honor than I am worth, for he touched
> me with his hand]

but he did not have the work read to him:

> Tant a l'en fait qu'il m'a falu
> Demourer seulet en la mue,
> De mousse et de pouldre velu
> Comme ung viez aiz qu'on ne remue.   (Ll. 145–48)

> [When all was said and done I was left all alone, as if moult-
> ing, covered with moss and dust like an old board that no
> one stirs.]

The book's author responded to its bitter complaint:

> Siques, mon filz, couche l'escu,
> Ferme le pié.
>
>   (Ll. 325–26)

> [Courage, my son, grip your shield tightly and brace your
> feet well.]

And the book did indeed take courage, shake its wings, and fly off
like a bird.

I Bibliography

Abbreviations

CFMA   Classiques français du Moyen Age
SATF   Société des anciens textes français
TLF   Textes littéraires français

Primary Texts and Authors

Adevineaux amoureux. In *Amorous Games: A Critical Edition of "Les Adevineaux Amoureux,"* edited by James Woodrow Hassell Jr. Publications of the American Folklore Society, Bibliographical and Special Series, no. 25. Austin, Texas: University of Texas Press, 1974.

Alexis, Guillaume. *Oeuvres poétiques.* Edited by Arthur Piaget and Emile Picot. SATF. 3 vols. Paris: Firmin-Didot, 1896–1908.

Amadas et Ydoine, roman du XIIIᵉ siècle. Edited by John R. Reinhard. CFMA, no. 51. Paris: Champion, 1926.

André le Chapelain. *Traité de l'amour courtois.* Translated by Claude Buridant. Bibliothèque française et romane, Séries D: Initiation, textes, et documents, no. 9. Paris: Klincksieck, 1974. Available in English as *The Art of Courtly Love,* edited by Frederick W. Locke, translated by John Jay Parry (New York: Frederick Unger, 1963). Also available as *De amore et amoris remedio: Andreas Capellanus on Love,* edited and translated by P. G. Walsh (London: Duckworth, 1982).

Aneau, Barthélemy. *L'Imagination poëtique.* Lyon, 1552.

Antitus. *Poésies.* Edited by Manuela Python. TLF, no. 422. Geneva: Droz, 1992.

Arnoul d'Orléans. *Allegoriae super Ovidii Metamorphosin.* In *Arnolfo d'Orléans, un cultore di Ovidio nel secolo XII,* by Fausto Ghisalberti. Memorie del Reale Istituto Lombardo di scienze e lettere, classe di lettere, scienze morali e storiche, vol. 24, ser. 3, no. 15, fasc. 4. Milan: Hoepli, 1932.

Bibliography

L'Atre périlleux, roman de la Table Ronde. Edited by Brian Woledge. CFMA, no. 76. Paris: Champion, 1936.

Avionnet. In vol. 2 of *Recueil général des Isopets,* edited by Julia Bastin. SATF. Paris: Champion, 1930.

Barton, John. *Donait françois.* In "Die ältesten Anleitungsschriften zur Erlernung der französischen Sprache," by Edmund Stengel. *Zeitschrift für neufranzösische Sprache und Literatur* 1 (1879): 1–40.

Benoît de Sainte-Maure. *Le Roman de Troie.* Edited on the basis of all known manuscripts by Léopold Constans. SATF. 6 vols. Paris: Firmin Didot, 1904–12.

Bernard de Ventadour. *Chansons d'amour.* Critical edition and translation by Moshe Lazar. Bibliothèque française et romane, Séries B: Editions critiques de textes, no. 4. Paris: Klincksieck, 1966. Available in English as *Songs,* edited by Stephen G. Nichols Jr. et al. (Chapel Hill: University of North Carolina Press, 1962).

Boccaccio, Giovanni. *De casibus virorum illustrium.* Edited by Pier Giorgio Ricci and Vittore Zaccaria. Vol. 9 of *Tutte le opere di Giovanni Boccaccio,* edited by Vittore Branca. Milan: Mondadori, 1983. Available in English as *The Fates of Illustrious Men,* translated by Louis Brewer Hall (New York: F. Ungar, 1965).

———. *De mulieribus claris.* Edited by Vittore Zaccaria. Vol. 10 of *Tutte le opere di Giovanni Boccaccio,* edited by Vittore Branca. Milan: Mondadori, 1967. Available in English as *Concerning Famous Women,* translated by Guido A. Guarino (New Brunswick: Rutgers University Press, 1963).

———. *Decameron.* Edited by Vittore Branca. 6th ed. 2 vols. Milan: Mondadori, 1995. Available in French as *Le Décaméron,* translated by Jean Bourciez, Classiques Garnier (Paris: Garnier, 1974, 1988). Available in English as *Decameron,* translated by John Payne, revised by Charles S. Singleton, 3 vols. (Berkeley: University of California Press, 1982).

Bouchet, Jean. *Les Annales d'Aquitaine.* Poitiers, France, 1524.

Bugnin, Jacques de. *Le Congié Pris du siècle séculier, poème du XVᵉ Siècle.* Edited by Arthur Piaget. Recueil de travaux publiés par la Faculté des Lettres de l'Université de Neuchâtel, no. 6. Paris: Imprimerie Attinger, 1916.

Caulier, Achille. *La Cruelle Femme en amour.* In pt. 4 of *"La Belle Dame sans mercy* et ses imitations," by Arthur Piaget. *Romania* 31 (1902): 315–49.

———. *L'Hôpital d'amour.* In pt. 11 of *"La Belle Dame sans mercy* et ses imitations," by Arthur Piaget. *Romania* 34 (1905): 559–65.

Les Cent Ballades, poème du XIVe siècle composé par Jean le Seneschal avec la collaboration de Philippe d'Artois, comte d'Eu, de Boucicaut le Jeune et de Jean de Crésecque. Edited by Gaston Raynaud. SATF. Paris: Firmin-Didot, 1905.

Champier, Symphorien. *La Nef des dames vertueuses.* Lyon, 1502, 1503; Paris, 1515, 1531.

Charles d'Orléans. *Poésies.* Edited by Pierre Champion. CFMA, nos. 34, 56. 2 vols. Paris: Champion, 1923–27. Available in English as *The Poems of Charles d'Orléans,* edited by Sally Purcell (Cheadle, Eng.: Carcanet Press, 1973). Also quoted from *The French Chansons of Charles d'Orléans.* Edited and translated by Sarah Spence. Garland Library of Medieval Literature, vol. 46, ser. A. New York: Garland, 1986.

Chartier, Alain. *La Belle Dame sans mercy et les poésies lyriques.* Edited by Arthur Piaget. TLF, no. 1. Paris: Droz, 1945. 2d ed., Geneva: Droz; Lille, France: Giard, 1949.

———. *Dialogus familiaris amici et sodalis super deploracione gallice calamitatis.* In *Les Oeuvres latines d'Alain Chartier,* critical edition by Pascale Bourgain-Hemeryck. Paris: Editions du Centre national de la recherche scientifique, 1977.

———. *Le Livre de l'esperance.* Edited by François Rouy. Bibliothèque du XVe siècle, no. 51. Paris: Champion, 1989.

———. *Poèmes.* Edited by James Cameron Laidlaw. 10/18, no. 1929. Paris: UGE, 1988. This volume contains *Le Livre des quatre dames, Le Debat de reveille matin, La Complainte, La Belle Dame sans mercy, Les Lectres des dames a Alain, La Requeste baillee aux dames contre Alain, L'Excusation aux dames, Le Breviaire des nobles, Le Lay de paix,* and *Le Debat du heraut, du vassault, et du villain.*

———. *The Poetical Works of Alain Chartier.* Edited by James Cameron Laidlaw. London: Cambridge University Press, 1974.

———. *Le Quadrilogue invectif.* Edited by Eugénie Droz. CFMA, no. 32. 2d ed. Paris: Champion, 1950.

Chastelain, Georges. *Le Temple de Bocace.* Edited by Susanna Bliggenstorfer. Romanica Helvetica, no. 104. Berne: Francke, 1988.

La Châtelaine de Vergy. Bilingual edition by Jean Dufournet and Liliane Dulac. Folio, no. 2576. Paris: Gallimard, 1994.

Chaucer, Geoffrey. *The Works.* Edited by F. N. Robinson. New Cambridge Edition. Boston: Houghton Mifflin, 1961.

Chrétien de Troyes. *Le Chevalier de la charrete.* Edited by Mario Roques. CFMA, no. 86. Paris: Champion, 1958, 1982. Available in English as

Lancelot, or, The Knight of the Cart, translated by Ruth Harwood Cline (Athens: University of Georgia Press, 1990). Also available in *The Complete Romances of Chrétien de Troyes,* translated by David Staines (Bloomington: Indiana University Press, 1990).

———. *Cligès.* Edited by Alexandre Micha. CFMA, no. 84. Paris: Champion, 1957. Available in English as *Cligés: A Romance,* translated by L. J. Gardiner (New York: Cooper Square, 1966). Also available in *The Complete Romances of Chrétien de Troyes,* translated by David Staines (Bloomington: Indiana University Press, 1990).

Christine de Pizan. *L'Advision Christine.* Edited by Christine Reno, with Liliane Dulac. Forthcoming.

———. *Lavision-Christine.* Edited by Sister Mary Louis Towner. Washington, D.C.: Catholic University of America Press, 1932. Available in English as *Christine's Vision,* translated by Glenda K. McLeod, Garland Library of Medieval Literature, vol. 68, ser. B (New York: Garland, 1993).

———. *Cent Ballades d'amant et de dame.* Edited by Jacqueline Cerquiglini. 10/18, no. 1529. Paris: UGE, 1982.

———. *Le Dit de la Rose.* In *Oeuvres poétiques.* Quoted from *The Writings of Christine de Pizan.* Edited and translated by Charity Cannon Willard. New York: Persea, 1994.

———. *L'Epistre Othea.* Edited by Halina Didycky Loukopoulos, in "Classical Mythology in the Works of Christine de Pisan, with an Edition of 'L'Epistre Othea' from the Manuscript Harley 4431." Ph.D. diss., Wayne State University, 1977. Available in English as *Letter of Othea to Hector,* translated by Jane Chance, Focus Library of Medieval Women (Newburyport, Mass.: Focus Info Group, 1989).

———. *Le Livre de la cité des dames.* In "Le Livre de la Cité des Dames," by Maureen C. Curnow. 2 vols. Ph.D. diss., Vanderbilt University, 1975. Available in English as *The Book of the City of Ladies,* translated by Earl J. Richards (New York: Persea Books, 1982).

———. *Le Livre de la mutacion de fortune.* Edited by Suzanne Solente. SATF. 4 vols. Paris: Picard, 1959–66.

———. *Le Livre des fais et bonnes meurs du sage roy Charles V.* Edited by Suzanne Solente. Société de l'Histoire de France. 2 vols. Paris: Champion, 1936–41. Some passages are available in English in *The Writings of Christine de Pizan,* edited and translated by Charity Cannon Willard (New York: Persea Books, 1994).

————. *Le Livre du chemin de long estude.* Edited by Robert Püschel. Berlin, 1881, 1887. Reprint, Paris: Slatkine, 1974.

————. *Le Livre du corps de policie.* Edited by Robert H. Lucas. TLF, no. 145. Geneva: Droz: 1967. Available in English as *The Book of the Body Politic,* edited and translated by Kate Langdon Forhan (Cambridge: Cambridge University Press, 1994).

————, *Oeuvres poétiques de Christine de Pisan.* Edited by Maurice Roy. SATF. 3 vols. Paris, 1886–96.

Commynes, Philippe de. *Mémoires.* Edited by Joseph Calmette. Les classiques de l'histoire de France au Moyen Age, nos. 3, 5, 6. 3 vols. Paris: Champion, 1924–25. Available in English as *The Memoirs of Philippe de Commynes,* edited by Samuel Kinser, translated by Isabelle Cazeaux, 2 vols. (Columbia: University of South Carolina Press, 1969–73).

La cour amoureuse dite de Charles VI. Vol. 1, *Armoiries et notices biographiques, 1–300,* and vol. 2, *Armoiries et notices biographiques, 301–700,* of the critical edition of the manuscript sources by Carla Bozzolo and Hélène Loyau. Paris: Léopard d'Or, 1982.

Courcy, Jean de. *Le Chemin de vaillance.* Edited by B. D. Dubuc, in "Etude critique et édition partielle du 'Chemin de vaillance' de Jean de Courcy d'après le manuscrit British Museum Royal, 14 E. II (French text)." Ph.D. diss., University of Connecticut, 1981. Ann Arbor, Mich.: University Microfilms International, 1981.

————. *Chronique de la Bouquechardière.* MS, Fonds français 329, Bibliothèque nationale, Paris. Quoted from "La Connaissance de l'Antiquité et le problème de l'humanisme en langue vulgaire dans la France du XVᵉ siècle," by J. Monfrin. In *The Late Middle Ages and the Dawn of Humanism outside Italy: Proceedings of the International Conference, Louvain, May 11–13, 1970,* edited by G. Verbeke and J. Ijsewijn, Mediaevalia Lovaniensia, ser. 1, studia 1. Louvain, Belgium: University Press; The Hague: Martinus Nijhoff, 1972.

Crétin, Guillaume. *Oeuvres poétiques de Guillaume Crétin.* Edited by Kathleen Chesney. Paris: Firmin-Didot, 1932.

Dante Alighieri. *Il Convivio.* Quoted from *Dante's Il Convivio (The Banquet).* Translated by Richard H. Lansing. Garland Library of Medieval Literature, vol. 65, ser. B. New York: Garland, 1990.

————. *Opere.* Edited by Vittore Branca, Francesco Maggini, and Bruno Nardi. Florence: F. Le Monnier, 1964. Available in French as

Oeuvres complètes, translated by André Pézard, Bibliothèque de la Pléiade (Paris: Gallimard, 1965).

———. *Vita nova.* Quoted from *The New Life of Dante Alighieri,* translated by Charles Eliot Norton. Boston, 1867.

Denis Foulechat, trans. *Tyrans, princes, et prêtres (Jean de Salisbury, Policratique IV et VIII).* Edited by Charles Brucker. Le Moyen Français, no. 21 (Montreal: CERES, 1987).

Des Périers, Bonaventure. *Cymbalum mundi.* Edited by Peter H. Nurse. Manchester, Eng.: University Press; Paris: D'Argences, 1958. Available with a preface by Michael A. Screech. Geneva: Droz, 1983. Available in English as *Cymbalum mundi: Four Very Ancient Joyous and Facetious Poetic Dialogues,* translated by Bettina L. Knapp (New York: Bookman Associates, 1965).

Diekstra, F. N. M., ed. and trans. "The Poetic Exchange between Philippe de Vitry and Jean de le Mote: A New Edition." *Neophilologus* 70 (1986): 504–19.

Les Douze Dames de rhétorique [par maistre Johan Robertet et alii]. Edited by Louis Batissier. Moulins, 1838.

Dufour, Antoine. *Les Vies des femmes célèbres.* Edited by G. Jeanneau. TLF, no. 168. Geneva: Droz, 1970.

Etienne de Conty. *Brevis tractatus.* MS, Fonds latin 11730, Bibliothèque nationale, Paris.

Eustache Deschamps. *Oeuvres complètes.* Edited by Marquis de Queux de Saint-Hilaire and Gaston Raynaud. SATF. 11 vols. Paris: Firmin-Didot, 1878–1903.

Fabri, Pierre. *Le Grant et vrai art de pleine rhétorique.* Edited by Alexandre Héron. 3 vols. Rouen, 1889–90. Reprint, Geneva: Slatkine, 1969.

Femina. In *The Teaching and Cultivation of the French Language in England during Tudor and Stuart Times; With an Introductory Chapter on the Preceding Period,* by Kathleen Rebillon Lambley. Manchester, Eng.: University Press; London: Longmans, Green, 1920.

Gautier de Coinci. *Les Miracles de Nostre Dame par Gautier de Coinci.* Edited by V. Frederic Koenig. TLF, nos. 64, 95, 131, 176. 4 vols. Geneva: Droz; Lille, France: Giard; Paris: Minard, 1955–70.

Gervaise. *Le Bestiaire.* In "Le Bestiaire de Gervaise," by P. Meyer. *Romania* 1 (1872): 420–43.

Gilles Li Muisis. *Poésies.* Edited by Baron Kervyn de Lettenhove. 2 vols. Louvain, Belgium, 1882.

Giraut de Bornelh. *Sämtliche Lieder des Trobadors Giraut de Bornelh.*

Edited by Adolf Kolsen. 2 vols. Halle, Germany: Niemeyer, 1910–35.

Gossouin. *L'Image du monde de Maître Gossouin.* Prose version edited by Oliver Herbert Prior. Lausanne: Payot, 1913.

Gréban, Arnoul. *Le Mystère de la Passion.* Critical edition by Omer Jodogne. Mémoires de l'Académie royale de Belgique, Classe des Lettres, coll. in-4°, ser. 2. 2 vols. Brussels: Académie royale de Belgique, 1965–83.

Gréban, Simon. *Complaincte de la mort de maistre Jacques Millet qui composa la Destruction de Troye.* Critical edition by Marc-René Jung and Claude Thiry. Forthcoming.

La Guerre de Metz en 1324. Edited by Ernest de Bouteiller. Paris, 1875.

Gui d'Ussel. *Les Poésies des quatre troubadours d'Ussel.* Edited by Jean Audiau. Paris: Delagrave, 1922.

Guillaume de Digulleville. *Le Pèlerinage de la vie humaine de Guillaume de Deguilleville.* Edited by J. J. Stürzinger. London, 1893. Available in English as *The Pilgrimage of Human Life,* translated by Eugene Clasby, Garland Library of Medieval Literature, vol. 76, ser. B (New York: Garland, 1992).

———. *Le Pèlerinage de l'âme de Guillaume de Deguilleville.* Edited by J. J. Stürzinger. London, 1895. Available in English as *The Pilgrimage of the Soul,* critical edition by Rosemarie Potz McGerr, Garland Medieval Texts, no. 16 (New York: Garland, 1990).

———. *Le Pèlerinage de Jésus-Christ de Guillaume de Deguilleville.* Edited by J. J. Stürzinger. London, 1897.

Guillaume de Lorris and Jean de Meun. *Le Roman de la Rose.* Edited by Félix Lecoy. CFMA, nos. 92, 95, 98. 3 vols. Paris: Champion, 1965–70. Available in English as *The Romance of the Rose,* translated by Charles Dahlberg (Hanover: University Press of New England, 1983). Also available as *The Romance of the Rose,* edited and translated by Frances Horgon (Oxford: Oxford University Press, 1994).

Guillaume de Machaut. *Le Dit de la Fonteinne amoureuse.* Edited and translated by Jacqueline Cerquiglini-Toulet. Moyen Age. Paris: Stock, 1993. Available in English as *The Fountain of Love (La Fonteinne Amoureuse) and Two Other Love Vision Poems,* edited and translated by R. Barton Palmer, Garland Library of Medieval Literature, vol. 54, ser. A (New York: Garland, 1993).

———. "The Dit de la harpe of Guillaume de Machaut." Edited by Karl Young. In *Essays in Honor of Albert Feuillerat.* New Haven: Yale University Press, 1943.

————. *Le Livre du Voir-Dit de Guillaume de Machaut où sont contées les amours de messire Guillaume de Machaut et de Péronelle, dame d'Armentières, avec les lettres et les réponses, les ballades, lais, et rondeaux dudit Guillaume et de ladite Péronelle.* Edited by Paulin Paris. Paris, 1875.

————. *Oeuvres.* Edited by Ernest Hoepffner. SATF. 3 vols. Paris: Firmin-Didot; Champion, 1908, 1911, 1921. *Le Remede de fortune* is quoted from *Le Jugement du roy de Behaingne and Remede de fortune.* Edited by James I. Wimsatt and William W. Kibler. Chaucer Library. Athens: University of Georgia Press, 1988. Works available in English include *Le Jugement dou roy de Behaingne: The Judgment of the King of Bohemia,* edited and translated by R. Barton Palmer, Garland Library of Medieval Literature, vol. 9, ser. A (New York: Garland, 1984); and *Le Jugement dou roy de Navarre: The Judgment of the King of Navarre,* edited and translated by R. Barton Palmer, Garland Library of Medieval Literature, vol. 45, ser. A (New York: Garland, 1988).

————. *Poésies lyriques.* Edited by V. Chichmaref [Vladimir Fedorovich Shishmarev]. 2 vols. Paris: Champion, 1909. Reprint, 2 vols. in 1, Geneva: Slatkine, 1973.

————. *La Prise d'Alexandrie ou chronique du roi Pierre Ier de Lusignan.* Edited by L. de Mas Latrie. Publications de la Société de l'Orient latin, Série historique, no. 1. Geneva, 1877.

Guillebert de Metz. *Description de la ville de Paris au XVe siècle.* Edited by [Antoine Jean Victor] Le Roux de Lincy. Paris, 1855.

Hugh of St. Victor. *Hugonis de Sancto Victore Didascalicon de studio legendi.* Critical text by Brother Charles Henry Buttimer. Studies in Medieval and Renaissance Latin, no. 10. Washington, D.C.: Catholic University of America Press, 1939. Available in English as *Didascalicon: A Medieval Guide to the Arts,* translated by Jerome Taylor (New York: Columbia University Press, 1962).

Huon de Méry. *Li Tornoiemenz Antecrit.* Edited by Georg Wimmer. Ausgaben und abhandlungen aus dem gebiete der romanischen Philologie, no. 76. Marburg, Germany, 1888. Available in French as *Le Tournoi de l'Antécrist (Li Tornoiemenz Antecrit),* edited by Georg Wimmer, translated by Stéphanie Orgeur (Orléans, France: Paradigme, 1994). See also *Le Torneiment Anticrist,* critical edition by Margaret O. Bender, Romance Monographs, no. 17 (University, Miss.: Romance Monographs, 1976).

Isidore of Seville. *Etymologiarum sive originum libri XX.* Edited by W. M.

Lindsay. Scriptorum classicorum Bibliotheca oxoniensis. 2 vols. Oxford: Oxford University Press, 1911.

———. *Etymologies.* Bk. 9, *Les Langues et les groupes sociaux.* Edited and translated by Marc Reydellet. Paris: Les Belles-Lettres, 1984.

Jacques de Longuyon. *Les Voeux du paon.* In *The Buik of Alexander or the Buik of the Most Noble and Valiant Conquerour Alexander the Grit, by John Barbour,* edited, together with the French originals (*Li Fuerres de Gadres* and *Les Voeux du paon*), by R. L. Graeme Ritchie. Scottish Text Society. 4 vols. Edinburgh: William Blackwood and Sons, 1925–29.

Jacques de Voragine. *La Légende dorée.* Translated by J.-B. M. Roze. G.F., nos. 132–33. 2 vols. Paris: Flammarion, 1967. Available in English as *The Golden Legend: Readings on the Saints,* by Jacobus de Voragine, translated by William Granger Ryan, 2 vols. (Princeton: Princeton University Press, 1993).

Jean Bodel. *La Chanson des Saisnes.* Critical edition by Annette Brasseur. TLF, no. 369. 2 vols. Geneva: Droz, 1989.

Jean Corbechon. *Le Livre des proprietez des choses.* MS, Fonds français 22531, Bibliothèque nationale, Paris.

Jean Courtecuisse. *Le Sermon sur la Passion.* Edited by Geneviève Hasenohr. Le Moyen Français, no. 16. Montreal: CERES, 1985.

Jean de Bueil. *Le Jouvencel par Jean de Bueil: Suivi du commentaire de Guillaume Tringant.* Edited and annotated by Léon Lecestre. Société de l'Histoire de France. 2 vols. Paris, 1887–89.

Jean de Condé. *Jean de Condé.* Vols. 2 and 3 of *Dits et contes de Baudouin de Condé et de son fils Jean de Condé,* by Auguste Scheler. Académie impériale et royale des sciences et belles-lettres. Brussels, 1866–67.

Jean de Garencières. *Le Chevalier Poète Jehan de Garencières (1372–1415): Sa Vie et ses poésies complètes dont de nombreuses inédites.* Edited by Young Abernathy Neal. 1 vol. in 2 pts. Paris: Nizet, 1953.

Jean de Le Mote. *Le Parfait du paon.* Critical edition by Richard J. Carey. Chapel Hill: University of North Carolina Press, 1972.

———. *Li Regret Guillaume, comte de Hainaut. Poëme inédit du XIVᵉ siècle.* Edited by Auguste Scheler. Louvain, Belgium, 1882.

———. *La Voie d'Enfer et de Paradis.* In *"La Voie d'Enfer et de Paradis": An Unpublished Poem of the Fourteenth Century by Jehan de le Mote,"* by Sister M. Aquiline Pety. Washington, D.C.: Catholic University of America Press, 1940.

Jean de Meun. *Le Roman de la Rose.* See Guillaume de Lorris and Jean de Meun.

Jean Froissart. *Ballades et rondeaux.* Edited by Rae S. Baudoin. TLF, no. 252. Geneva and Paris: Droz, 1978.

———. *Chroniques.* Bks. 1–3. Edited by Simeon Luce, Gaston Reynaud, Léon Mirot, and Albert Mirot. Société de l'Histoire de France. Paris, 1869–1975.

———. *Chroniques.* Bk. 4. Edited by Kervyn de Lettenhove. In vol. 15 of *Oeuvres de Froissart.* Brussels, 1871. The *Chroniques* are available in English as *Froissart's Chronicles,* edited and translated by John Jolliffe (New York: Modern Library/Random House, 1968).

———. *"Dits" et "Débats."* Edited by Anthime Fourrier. TLF, no. 274. Geneva: Droz, 1979.

———. *L'Espinette amoureuse.* Edited by Anthime Fourrier. 2d ed. Paris: Klincksieck, 1972.

———. *Le Joli Buisson de Jonece.* Edited by Anthime Fourrier. TLF, no. 222. Geneva: Droz, 1975.

———. *Meliador.* Edited by Auguste Longnon. SATF. 3 vols. Paris, 1895–99.

———. *Poésies.* Edited by Auguste Scheler. 3 vols. Brussels: 1869–72. Reprinted in 3 vols. as *Oeuvres de Froissart: Poésies,* Geneva: Slatkine, 1977.

———. *La Prison amoureuse.* Edited by Anthime Fourrier. Bibliothèque française et romane, Séries B: Editions critiques de textes, no. 13. Paris: Klincksieck, 1974.

Jean Le Court, dit Brisebare. *Brisebarre: Le Plait de l'evesque et de droit.* Edition critique du manuscrit ancien fonds royal n° 2061–64° de la Bibliothèque royale de Copenhague, by Jonna Kjaer. Romance Studies of the University of Copenhagen. *Revue Romane,* no. 10. Copenhagen: Akademisk Forlag, 1977.

———. *Le Restor du paon [par] Jean Le Court di Brisebare.* Critical edition by Richard J. Carey. TLF, no. 119. Geneva: Droz, 1966.

Jean Le Fèvre. *Les Lamentations de Matheolus et le Livre de leesce de Jehan le Fèvre de Ressons.* Critical edition by A. G. van Hamel. Bibliothèque de l'Ecole des hautes études, Sciences historiques et Philologiques, nos. 95, 96. 2 vols. Paris, 1895.

———. *Le Respit de la Mort par Jean le Fevre.* Edited by G. Hasenohr-Esnos. SATF. Paris: Picard, 1969.

———. *La Vieille ou les dernières Amours d'Ovide, poëme français du XIVᵉ siècle.* Translated from the Latin of Richard de Fournival by Jean Le Fèvre. Edited by Hippolyte Cocheris. Paris, 1861.

Jean Renart. *Le Roman de la Rose ou de Guillaume de Dole.* Edited by Félix Lecoy. CFMA, no. 91. Paris: Champion, 1962. Available in English as *The Romance of the Rose, or, Guillaume de Dole,* translated by Patricia Terry and Nancy Vine Durling (Philadelphia: University of Pennsylvania Press, 1993).

Le Jeu d'Adam (Ordo representacionis Ade). Edited by Willem Noomen. CFMA, no. 99. Paris: Champion, 1971. Available in English, adapted, as *Adam: A Religious Play of the Twelfth Century,* translated by Edward Noble Stone (Seattle: University of Washington Press, 1928).

John of Salisbury. *Metalogicon (Ioannis Saresberiensis Metalogicon).* Edited by Clemens Webb. Oxford: Clarendon Press, 1929. Available in English as *The Metalogicon of John of Salisbury: A Twelfth-Century Defense of the Verbal and Logical Arts of the Trivium,* edited and translated by Daniel D. McGarry. 1955; Gloucester, Mass.: Peter Smith, 1971).

———. *Policraticus.* See Denis Foulechat.

La Marche, Olivier de. *Mémoires d'Olivier de La Marche.* Edited by Henri Beaune and Jules d'Arbaumont. Société de l'Histoire de France. 3 vols. Paris, 1883–85.

La Sale, Antoine de. *Jehan de Saintré.* Edited by Jean Misrahi and Charles A. Knudson. TLF, no. 117. Geneva: Droz; Paris: Minard, 1965. Available in English as *Little John of Saintré: Le petit Jehan de Saintré by Antoine de La Sale c. 1368–1462,* translated by Irvine Gray (London: G. Routledge & Sons, 1931).

———. *Le Reconfort de Madame de Fresne.* Edited by Ian Hill. Exeter, Eng.: University of Exeter Press, 1979.

———. *La Salade.* Vol. 1 of *Oeuvres complètes,* critical edition by Fernand Desonay. Bibliothèque de la Faculté de philosophie et lettres de l'Université de Liège, no. 68. Liège: Faculté de philosophie et lettres; Paris: Droz, 1935.

———. *La Sale.* Vol. 2 of *Oeuvres complètes,* critical edition by Fernand Desonay. Bibliothèque de la Faculté de philosophie et lettres de l'Université de Liège, no. 92. Paris: Droz, 1941.

Latini, Brunetto. *Li Livres dou tresor.* Critical edition by Francis J. Carmody. University of California Publications in Modern Philology, no. 22. Berkeley: University of California Press, 1948. Available in English as *The Book of the Treasure,* translated by Paul Barrette and Spurgeon Baldwin (New York: Garland, 1993).

Le Franc, Martin. *Le Champion des dames.* Edited by Arthur Piaget. Mémoires et documents, Société d'histoire de la Suisse romande, ser. 3, vol. 8, ll. 1–8144. Lausanne: Payot, 1968. Quotations from the unpublished portion of this work are taken from MS, Fonds français 12476, Bibliothèque nationale, Paris.

———. *Complainte du livre du Champion des dames a maistre Martin Le Franc son acteur.* Edited by Gaston Paris, in "Un Poème inédit de Martin Le Franc," *Romania* 16 (1887): 383–437.

Legrand, Jacques. *Archiloge Sophie: Livre de bonnes meurs.* Critical edition by Evencio Beltran. Geneva: Slatkine; Paris: Champion, 1986. Translated into English as *The Book of Good Manners* (Westminster, Eng.: William Caxton, 1497).

Lemaire de Belges, Jean. *Les Illustrations de Gaule et singularitez de Troye.* Vol. 1 of *Oeuvres,* edited by J. Stecher. Louvain, Belgium, 1882. Reprint, Geneva: Slatkine, 1969.

Lexique latin-français. MS, Fonds latin 13032, Bibliothèque nationale, Paris. Translated from the lexicon inserted by Giovanni Balbi in his *Catholicon.* In *Lexiques alphabétiques,* vol. 1, pt. 2 of *Recueil général des lexiques français du Moyen Age (XIIᵉ–XVᵉ siècles),* edited by Mario Roques. (Paris: Champion, 1938).

Le Livre du Chevalier de La Tour Landry pour l'enseignement de ses filles. Edited by Anatole de Montaiglon. Bibliothèque elzévirienne, no. 36. Paris, 1854. Available in English as *The Book of the Knight of La Tour-Landry,* edited by Thomas Wright (London: Published for the Early English Text Society by Kegan Paul, Trench, Trübner, 1906).

La Manière de langage qui enseigne à bien parler et écrire le français. In *La Manière de langage qui enseigne à bien parler et à écrire le français: Modèles de conversation composés en Angleterre à la fin du XIVᵉ siècle,* edited by Jacques Gessler. Brussels: L'Edition Universelle; Paris: Droz, 1934.

Marguerite Porete. *Le Mirouer des simples ames anienties et qui seulement demourent en vouloir et desir d'amour.* Edited by Romana Guarnieri. Rome: Edizioni di Storia e Letteratura, 1961. Available in English as *The Mirror of Simple Souls,* translated by Ellen L. Babinsky (New York: Paulist Press, 1993).

Marie de France. *Les Lais.* Edited by Jean Rychner. CFMA, no. 93. Paris: Champion, 1966. Available in English as *The Lais of Marie de France,* translated by Glyn S. Burgess and Keith Busby (Harmondsworth, Eng.: Penguin Books, 1986). Also available as *Marie de France: Seven of Her Lays Done into English,* translated by Edith Rickert (New York: New Amsterdam, 1901).

Martial d'Auvergne. *Les Arrêts d'Amour de Martial d'Auvergne.* Edited by Jean Rychner. SATF. Paris: Picard, 1951.

Matteo Villani. *Cronica di Matteo Villani a miglior lezione ridotta.* 2 vols. Florence, 1846.

Meschinot, Jean. *Les Lunettes des princes.* Edited by Christine Martineau-Génieys. Publications romanes et françaises, no. 121. Geneva: Droz, 1972.

Michault, Pierre. *Le Doctrinal du temps present* (1466). Edited by Thomas Walton. Paris: Droz, 1931.

Michault Taillevent. *Le Passe Temps.* In *Un Poète Bourgignon du XVᵉ siècle: Michault Taillevent,* edited by Robert Deschaux. Publications romanes et françaises, no. 132. Geneva: Droz, 1975.

Molinet, Jean. *Les Faicts et dictz de Jean Molinet.* Edited by Noël Dupire. 3 vols. Paris: SATF, 1936–39.

Montaigne, Michel Eyquem de. *Essais.* Edited by Albert Thibaudet. Bibliothèque de la Pléiade, no. 14. Paris: Gallimard, 1937. Quoted from *The Essays of Michel de Montaigne.* Edited and translated by Jacob Zeitlin. New York: Alfred A. Knopf, 1934.

Nicole Oresme. *Le Livre de Ethiques d'Aristote.* Edited by Albert Douglas Menut from the text of MS 2902, Bibliothèque Royale de Belgique. New York: Stechert, 1940.

Oton de Grandson. *Oton de Grandson: Sa Vie et ses poésies.* Edited by Arthur Piaget. Mémoires et documents, Société d'histoire de la Suisse romande, ser. 3, vol. 1. Lausanne: Payot, 1941.

Ovide moralisé, poème du commencement du quatorzième siècle. Edited, on the basis of all known manuscripts, by Cornelis De Boer. Verhandelingen der Koninklijke Nederlandsche Akademie van Wetenschappen, Afdeeling Letterkunde, Nieuwe Reeks, nos. 15, 21, 30/3, 37, and 43. 5 vols. Amsterdam: J. Müller, 1915–38. The tale of Philomena and Procné is available in English in *Three Ovidian Tales of Love,* edited and translated by Raymond Cormier, Garland Library of Medieval Literature, vol. 26, ser. A (New York: Garland, 1986).

Petrarca, Francesco. *De l'Abondance des livres et de la réputation des écrivains.* Translated from the Latin by Victor Develay. Paris, 1883. Available in English as "On the Abondance of Books," ed. and trans. Conrad Rawski.

————. *Francisci Petrarchae opera.* 3 vols. Basel, 1554.

————. *Lettres de François Pétrarque à Jean Boccace.* Translated from the Latin by Victor Develay. Paris: Flammarion, 1911. Quoted from *Letters of Old Age: Rerum senilium libri I–XVIII.* Translated by Aldo S. Bernardo, Saul Levin, and Reta A. Bernardo. 2 vols. Baltimore: Johns Hopkins University Press, 1992. Also quoted from *Letters on Familiar Matters: Rerum familiarus libri XVII–XXIV.* Translated by Aldo S. Bernardo. 3 vols. Baltimore: Johns Hopkins University Press, 1985. English translations are available of many of Petrarch's letters in, among others, *Letters,* edited and translated by Morris Bishop (Bloomington: Indiana University Press, 1966).

————. "On the Abundance of Books." In *Petrarch: Four Dialogues for Scholars.* Edited and translated by Conrad H. Rawski. Cleveland: Press of Western Reserve University, 1967.

————. *Pétrarque et la pensée latine: Tradition et novation en littérature.* Edited and translated by Alain Michel. Avignon: Aubanel, 1974.

————. *Sine nomine: Lettere polemiche e politiche.* Edited by Ugo Dotti. Rome: Laterza, 1974.

Philippe de Mézières. *Le Songe du vieil pelerin.* Edited by George William Coopland. 2 vols. Cambridge: Cambridge University Press, 1969.

Philippe de Vitry. See Diekstra.

Pierre de Beauvais. *Le Bestiaire de Pierre de Beauvais: Version courte.* Edited by Guy R. Mermier. Paris: Nizet, 1977.

Pierre de Hauteville. *La Complainte de l'amant trespassé de deuil. L'Inventaire des biens demourez du decés de l'amant trespassé de deuil de Pierre de Hauteville.* Edited by Rose M. Bidler. Le Moyen Français, no. 18. Montreal: CERES, 1986.

————. *La Confession et testament de l'amant trespassé de deuil de Pierre de Hauteville.* Edited by Rose M. Bidler. Inedita et Rara, no. 1. Montreal: CERES, 1982.

Plato. *Phaedrus.* Translated with introduction and commentary by R. Hackforth. Cambridge: Cambridge University Press, 1952.

Proverbes français antérieurs au XVᵉ siècle. Edited by Joseph Morawski. CFMA, no. 47. Paris: Champion, 1925.

La Queste del Saint Graal. Edited by Albert Pauphilet. CFMA, no. 33. Paris: Champion, 1923. Available in English as *The Quest of the Holy Grail,* translated from the Old French by William Wistar Comfort (London: J. M. Dent & Sons, 1926). Also available as *The Quest of the Holy Grail,* translated by P. M. Matarasso (Baltimore: Penguin Books, 1969).

Les Règles de la seconde rhétorique. In *Recueil d'arts de seconde rhétorique,* edited by Ernest Langlois. Collection des documents inédits sur l'Histoire de France. Paris: Imprimerie nationale, 1902. Reprint, Geneva: Slatkine, 1974.

Regnier, Jean. *Les Fortunes et adversitez de Jean Regnier.* Edited by Eugénie Droz. SATF. Paris: Champion, 1923.

Regnier, Mathurin. *Oeuvres complètes.* Paris, 1853.

René d'Anjou. *Le Livre du Cuer d'Amours espris.* Edited by Susan Wharton. 10/18, no. 1385. Paris: UGE, 1980.

Richard de Bury (Richard Aungerville). *The Love of Books: The Philobiblon of Richard de Bury.* Edited by M. MacLagan. Translated by E. C. Thomas. Oxford: Published for the Shakespeare Head Press by Basil Blackwell, 1960. New York: Cooper Square Publishers, 1966.

Richard de Fournival. *Li Bestiaires d'Amours di Maistre Richart de Fornival e li response du Bestiaire.* Edited by Cesare Segre. Documenti di filologia, no. 2. Milan: Riccardo Ricciardi, 1957. For a more recent edition with Italian translation, see *Il Bestiario d'amore et la risposta al Bestiario,* edited by Francesco Zambon, Biblioteca medievale, no. 1 (Parma: Pratiche, 1987). Available in English as *Master Richard's Bestiary of Love and Response,* translated by Jeannette Beer (Berkeley: University of California Press, 1986).

Rodríguez del Padrón, Juan. *El Triunfo de las donas.* In *Obras de Juan Rodríguez de la Cámara (ó del Padrón),* edited by A. Paz y Melia. Madrid, 1884. In French, *Le Triomphe des Dames* (Paris, ca. 1498).

Le Roman de Troie en prose. MS, Fonds français 1627, Bibliothèque nationale, Paris.

Li Romans de Witasse le Moine, roman du XIIIᵉ siècle. Edited from MS, Fonds français 1553, Bibliothèque nationale, Paris, by Denis Joseph Conlon. Department of Romance Languages Studies in the Romance Languages and Literatures, no. 126. Chapel Hill: University of North Carolina Press, 1972.

Saint-Gelais, Octovien de (attributed to). *La Chasse d'amours.* Edited by Mary Beth Winn. TLF, no. 322. Geneva: Droz, 1984.

Sébillet, Thomas. *L'Art poétique français.* In *Traités de poétique et de rhétorique de la Renaissance,* edited by Francis Goyet. Le Livre de poche. Paris: Librairie générale française, 1990.

Bibliography

Le Songe du vergier. Edited by Marion Schnerb-Lièvre. 2 vols. Paris: Editions du Centre national de la recherche scientifique, 1982.

Tory, Geofroy. *Champ Fleury ou l'art et science de la proportion des lettres.* Photoreproduction of the princeps edition, Paris, 1529. Edited by Gustave Cohen. Paris: Bosse, 1931. Reprint (with new preface and a bibliography by K. Reichenberger and T. Berchem), Geneva: Slatkine, 1973. Available in English as *Champ fleury,* edited and translated by George B. Ives (New York: Grolier Club, 1927).

Villon, François. *Le Lais Villon et les poèmes variés.* Edited by Jean Rychner and Albert Henry. TLF, nos. 239, 240. 2 vols. Geneva: Droz, 1977. Available in English in *Complete Works,* edited and translated by Anthony Bonner (New York: McKay, 1960).

————. *Le Testament Villon.* Edited by Jean Rychner and Albert Henry. TLF, nos. 207, 208. 2 vols. Geneva: Droz, 1974. Available in English in *The Poems of François Villon,* translated by Galway Kinnell (Boston: Houghton Mifflin, 1977). Also available in *Complete Works,* edited and translated by Anthony Bonner (New York: McKay, 1960).

Watriquet de Couvin. *Dits de Watriquet de Couvin.* Edited by Auguste Scheler. Brussels, 1868.

Studies

Badel, Pierre-Yves. *Le Roman de la Rose au XIVᵉ siècle: Etude de la réception de l'oeuvre.* Geneva: Droz, 1980.

Baxandall, Michael. *Giotto and the Orators: Humanist Observers of Painting in Italy and the Discovery of Pictorial Composition, 1350–1450.* Oxford: Clarendon Press, 1971. In French, *Les Humanistes à la découverte de la composition en peinture (1340–1450)* (Paris: Seuil, 1989).

Beaune, Colette. *Naissance de la nation France.* Paris: Gallimard, 1985. Available in English as *The Birth of an Ideology: Myths and Symbols of Nation in Late-Medieval France,* edited by Fredric L. Cheyette, translated by Susan Ross Huston (Berkeley: University of California Press, 1991).

Cazelles, Raymond. *Jean l'Aveugle, comte de Luxembourg, roi de Bohême.* Bourges: Tardy, 1947.

Cerquiglini, Jacqueline. *"Un Engin si soutil": Guillaume de Machaut et l'écriture au XIVᵉ siècle.* Bibliothèque du XVᵉ siècle, no. 47. Geneva: Slatkine; Paris, Champion, 1985.

Correl, I. *Gottvater, Untersuchungen über seine bildichen Darstellungen bis zum Tridentinum.* Dissertation, University of Heidelberg, 1958.

Curtius, Ernst Robert. *Europäische Literatur und lateinisches Mittelalter.* Bern: A. Francke, 1948. In French, *La Littérature européenne et le Moyen Age latin,* translated by Jean Bréjoux (1956); 2 vols., Paris: Presses-Pocket, 1986. Available in English as *European Literature and the Latin Middle Ages,* translated by Willard R. Trask (Princeton: Princeton University Press, 1967).

Demats, Paule. *Fabula: Trois Etudes de mythographie antique et médiévale.* Publications romanes et françaises, no. 122. Geneva: Droz, 1973.

Didron, Adolphe Napoléon. *Iconographie chrétienne: Histoire de Dieu.* Paris, 1843. Available in English as *Christian Iconography; or, The History of Christian Art in the Middle Ages,* translated by E. J. Millington, additions and appendix by Margaret Stokes, 2 vols. (London, 1886).

Diez, Friedrich Christian. *Uber die Minnhöfe.* Berlin, 1825. In French, *Essai sur les Cours d'Amour,* translated by Ferdinand de Roisin (Paris, 1842).

Dumézil, Georges. *Apollon sonore et autres essais: Vingt-cinq esquisses de mythologie.* Paris: Gallimard, 1982. 2d ed., 1987.

Gilson, Etienne. "Le Moyen Age comme '*Saeculum modernum*.'" In *Concetto, storia, miti e immagini del Medio Evo,* edited by Vittore Branca. Venice: Sansoni, 1973.

Guenée, Bernard. *Entre l'Eglise et l'etat: Quatre vies de prélats français à la fin du Moyen Age, XIIIe–XVe siècle.* Bibliothèque des histoires. Paris: Gallimard, 1987. Available in English as *Between Church and State: The Lives of Four French Prelates in the Late Middle Ages,* translated by Arthur Goldhammer (Chicago: University of Chicago Press, 1991).

Huizinga, Johan. *Herfsttij der Middeleeuwen.* In French, *L'Automne du Moyen Age,* translated from the Dutch by Julia Bastin. 1932. Reprint, Paris: Payot, 1980. Available in English as *The Autumn of the Middle Ages,* translated by Rodney J. Payton and Ulrich Mammitzsch (Chicago: University of Chicago Press, 1996).

Jung, Marc-René. *Etudes sur le poème allégorique en France au Moyen Age.* Berne: Francke, 1971.

Kantorowicz, Ernst H. "La Souvereineté de l'artiste: Note sur quelques maximes juridiques et les théories de l'art à la Renaissance." In *Mourir pour la patrie.* Paris: Presses Universitaires de France, 1984. Available in English as "The Sovereignty of the Artist: A Note on

Legal Maxims and Renaissance Theories of Art," in *Selected Studies* (Locust Valley, N.Y.: J. J. Augustin, 1965).

Kris, Ernst, and Otto Kurz. *Die Legende vom künster.* . . . Vienna: Krystall Verlag, 1934. Available in English as *Legend, Myth, and Magic in the Image of the Artist: An Historical Experiment,* translated by Alastair Laing, revised by Lotte M. Newman (New Haven: Yale University Press, 1979). Available in French as *L'Image de l'artiste: Légende, mythe et magie: Un Essai historique,* translated from the English by Michèle Hechter (Paris: Rivages, 1987).

Krynen, Jacques. *Idéal du prince et pouvoir royal en France à la fin du Moyen Age (1380–1440): Etude de la littérature politique du temps.* Paris: Picard, 1981.

Leclercq, Dom Jean. *L'Amour des lettres et le désir de Dieu: Initiation aux auteurs monastiques du Moyen Age.* Paris: Editions du Cerf, 1957; 3d ed., 1990. Available in English as *The Love of Learning and the Desire for God: A Study of Monastic Culture,* translated by Catharine Misrahi, 3d ed. (New York: Fordham University Press, 1982).

Lusignan, Serge. *Parler vulgairement: Les Intellectuels et la langue française aux XIIIe et XIVe siècles.* Montreal: Presses de l'Université; Paris: Vrin, 1986.

Mâle, Emile. *L'Art religieux de la fin du Moyen Age en France: Etude sur l'iconographie du Moyen Age et sur ses sources d'inspiration* (1908). 5th ed. Paris: A. Colin, 1949. Available in English as *Religious Art in France in the Late Middle Ages: A Study of Medieval Iconography and its Sources,* edited by Harry Bober, translated by Marthiel Mathews (Princeton: Princeton University Press, 1986).

Michelet, Jules. *Journal.* Vol. 2. Edited by Paul Viallaneix. Paris: Gallimard, 1962.

———. *Le Moyen Age.* Bks. 1–17 of *Histoire de France.* Collection Bouquins. Paris: Laffont, 1981.

Paris, Gaston. "Les Cours d'amour au Moyen Age." *Journal des Savants* (1888): 664–75, 727–36.

Piaget, Arthur. "La *Belle Dame sans mercy* et ses imitations." Pt. 1, "La *Belle Dame sans mercy* et ses imitations." *Romania* 30 (1901): 22–48. Pt. 2, "*Le Parlement d'Amour* de Baudet Herenc." *Romania* 30 (1901): 317–20. Pt. 3, "*La Dame loyale en amours.*" *Romania* 30 (1901): 321–51. Pt. 4, "*La Cruelle Femme en amour* d'Achille Caulier." *Romania* 31 (1902): 315–49. Pt. 5, "*Les Erreurs du jugement de la belle dame sans mercy.*" *Romania* 33 (1904): 179–99. Pt. 6, "*La Belle Dame qui eut merci."* *Romania* 33 (1904): 200–6. Pt. 7, *"Dialogue d'un amoureux et de sa dame."* *Romania* 33 (1904): 206–8. Pt. 8, *"Le Jugement du povre triste amant banny."* *Romania* 34 (1905): 375–411. Pt. 9, *"Les Erreurs du jugement de l'amant banny."* *Romania* 34 (1905): 412–16. Pt. 10, *"Amant rendu cordelier à l'observance d'Amours."* *Romania* 34 (1905): 416–18. Pt. 11, *"L'Hôpital d'Amour,* par Achille Caulier." *Romania* 34 (1905): 559–65. Pt. 12, *"Le Traité de réveille qui dort."* *Romania* 34 (1905): 565–70. Pt. 13, *"Le Débat sans conclusion."* *Romania* 34 (1905): 570–74. Pt. 14, *"Le Desconseillé d'Amours."* *Romania* 34 (1905): 575–77. Pt. 15, *"Le Loyal Amant refusé."* *Romania* 34 (1905): 577–79. Pt. 16, *"La Desserte du desloyal."* *Romania* 34 (1905): 579–81. Pt. 17, *"La Sépulture d'Amour."* *Romania* 34 (1905): 581–82. Pt. 18, *"Le Martyr d'Amour* par Franci." *Romania* 34 (1905): 583–85. Pt. 19, *"Le Débat de la dame et de l'écuyer."* *Romania* 34 (1905): 585–89. Pt. 20, "Poèmes divers." *Romania* 34 (1905): 589–91. Pt. 21, "Conclusion." *Romania* 34 (1905): 591–602.

————. "La Cour Amoureuse, dite de Charles VI." *Romania* 20 (1891): 417–54.

Roudaut, Jean. *Autre Part: Paysages d'accompagnement.* Paris: Gallimard, 1979.

Spitzer, Leo. "Résonances: A propos du Mot *Stimmung." Nouvelle Revue de Psychanalyse* 32 (1985): 239–55.

Index

Library of Congress Cataloging-in-Publication Data

Cerquiglini-Toulet, Jacqueline.
    [Couleur de la mélancolie. English]
    The color of melancholy : the uses of books in the fourteenth century /
Jacqueline Cerquiglini-Toulet : translated by Lydia G. Cochrane.
        p.   cm. — (Parallax)
    Includes bibliographical references (p.   ) and index.
    ISBN 0-8018-5381-8 (alk. paper)
    1. French literature—To 1500—History and criticism.   2. Civilization,
Medieval—14th century.   3. Melancholy in literature.   I. Title.   II. Series:
Parallax (Baltimore, Md.)
PQ155.M52C4713   1997
840.9'353—dc21   97-5043
                                                                               CIP